How to Double and Triple
the Useful Life
of Everything You Own

HERBERT F. HOLTJE

& JOHN STOCKWELL

*Illustrated with photographs taken
specifically for this book*

Prentice-Hall, Inc.

Englewood Cliffs, New Jersey

Prentice-Hall International, Inc., *London*
Prentice-Hall of Australia, Pty. Ltd., *Sydney*
Prentice-Hall of Canada, Ltd., *Toronto*
Prentice-Hall of India Private Ltd., *New Delhi*
Prentice-Hall of Japan, Inc., *Tokyo*
Prentice-Hall of Southeast Asia Pte. Ltd., *Singapore*
Whitehall Books, Ltd., *Wellington, New Zealand*

Library of Congress Cataloging in Publication Data

Holtje, Herbert.
   How to double and triple the useful life of everything
you own.

   Includes index.
   1. Home economics. I. Stockwell, John, joint
author. II. Title.
TX147.H744   640'.2   76-58881

OTHER BOOKS BY HOLTJE & STOCKWELL:

How to Borrow Everything You Need to Build a Great Personal Fortune. Parker Publishing Company, Inc., 1974.

100 Ways to Make Money in Your Spare Time, Starting with Less than $100. Parker Publishing Company, Inc., 1972.

How This Book
Will Save You Money

Add up the cost of everything you own—home, car, furniture, appliances, clothing, sports and hobby equipment, and everything else—and what do you come up with?

A fortune!

Most people don't realize how much they have invested in all their possessions until some tragedy like a fire or a flood takes everything away from them all at once. Then they realize to their horror how much money it will take to replace all the things they use in day-to-day living.

Fortunately, most people do not have to live through such a terrible event, and most of us are foresighted enough to carry insurance policies that will take the financial brunt in case tragedy does strike.

Yet, strange as it may seem, most people literally suffer the equivalent of a "fire" or "flood" a little bit at a time. Most people don't know the quick, simple steps to take that will prolong—yes, even double and triple—the useful life of everything they may own.

If you can increase the life of everything you own—get much more use from it before it wears out—you won't replace your possessions nearly as quickly. Over a period of years, you can, in effect, save the fortune you would spend in replacing your possessions bit by bit.

On the other hand, by neglecting these simple steps, your possessions wear out much sooner. In the end, you wind up replacing everything you own more often than you would if you knew the secret of making things last. It's just as if you lost everything in a fire or flood—and without any insurance policy to help cover the loss.

What kind of secrets are we talking about that can be so enormously valuable to you in saving money every day? Here are some examples:

- a few drops of oil in the right place at the right time can keep your furnace working efficiently season after season— to say nothing of the annoyance of having a chilly breakdown in the middle of a cold, January night.
- once a month you can spend two or three extra minutes as you vacuum the house and save on expensive fuel bills, cut down on your electric bills, and probably add a year or more to the life of your refrigerator and freezer.
- with nothing more elaborate than a pad and pencil in the glove compartment, you can add thousands of carefree miles to your car, and drive with a new peace of mind.
- the "30-second check" of your lawnmower before you mow the lawn can make your mower last longer, save gas, and make your mowing job easier and faster.
- a dollar or two spent on lumber and dowels, plus the simplest tools, will help you store expensive sports equipment properly, and get extra seasons of enjoyment from skis, skates, fishing gear, tennis rackets, and the like.
- a few minutes spent on a simple task can double the life of your expensive rugs or give years of extra service from a hardwood floor.
- the "oil can and screwdriver" tour of your home that can add immeasurably to your enjoyment of your house, and prevent many costly repair bills.

In addition to all these little things that can be so important, there are equally important little things that you should never do, if you want to prevent trouble. Again, there are hints about—

- never allowing surfaces such as porcelain, tile, plastic, laminates, and similar materials to go untreated, so that damage and premature replacement can be prevented.
- never handling tools so that the edges get blunt. Keep them sharp and clean so you can work faster, safer, longer.

- never installing appliances incorrectly. Moving a refrigerator two inches one way or the other can make it work harder, waste electricity, and wear out years before its time.

These few examples should prove how valuable any of these techniques can be in saving you money, time and effort. And they are not hard to learn or to remember. By following the simple instructions you find in this book, you will find yourself observing these common-sense rules every time you work or play, every time you handle, use, or store any of the possessions you spent good money for, and which usually have much longer useful lives than you may have imagined.

At this point, we have to make one thing clear: we have no intention of turning you and your family into a bunch of stingy fanatics, putting patch upon patch, turning down thermostats and turning off lights. This type of economy becomes an obsession and soon every comfort is sacrificed toward the goal of saving every penny.

No, this is not a book for Scrooge's library. Rather, we think it is perfectly possible to enjoy yourself and continue to do all the things you are doing now. You should get all the enjoyment out of the things you own. All we will be doing is to show you the very easy things you can do to prolong the enjoyment of your possessions.

If you get three years of enjoyable use from a sixty dollar tennis racket, then each year has cost you twenty dollars. On the other hand, if you can get six years of enjoyment from the same racket, then each year has only cost you ten dollars. Your enjoyment hasn't been diminished...you haven't made a spectacle of yourself on the courts. All you have done is to save ten dollars a year by not having to replace that racket so soon. Multiply this simple example by the dozens of other things that you own and which might be wearing out prematurely, and the savings can become dazzling.

To make this book as easy to use as possible, we've broken it up into chapters that cover the main classes of your possessions—your home, car, furnishings, hobby equipment, and the like. With each chapter, we've arranged the most common articles in alphabetical sequence. Therefore, whether you're interested in the brakes on your car, the toaster in your kitchen, or a picnic bench on the patio, you can quickly find out the tested hints, procedures, and precautions you should take that will lengthen the useful life of everything you own.

Finally, we want to stress the fact that this is not a repair or fix-it book. You need no special training to use this book simply because little mechanical ability is required. Most of the procedures we describe can be understood and performed by a child. In fact, we recommend that you show them to your children as the best way of teaching them the proper way of taking care of things early in life.

All of these helps are here for just one purpose—to help you double and triple the enjoyment of everything you own now and will acquire in the future.

Herbert F. Holtje
John Stockwell

Table of Contents

Chapter 1

Inside and Out:

How to protect and preserve surfaces and everything that moves.

Household surfaces are probably more abused and less cared for than any other part of your home. However, most of these surfaces don't show the abuse as readily as other possessions that receive as much wear. But, when the wear does take its toll, it often becomes quite costly to put these surfaces back in shape. This first chapter is a guide to the care and preservation of most surfaces and materials found in a modern home.

CARING FOR HOME SURFACES

The first part of the chapter is an alphabetical listing of major surfaces, with details of what can be done to make them look better and last longer.

Aluminum. Aluminum is a relatively soft metal that can be bent, nicked, and dented quite easily. It also oxidizes—gets a powdery surface—when exposed to the elements. Aluminum pots and pans are covered in a later chapter, but aluminum surfaces such as those found in storm windows can benefit from occasional brightening with a fine grade of steel wool. Rub lightly, in one direction, and dust off the loosened oxide. One or two coats of liquid or paste wax will help keep aluminum surfaces bright for a long time. You can also apply a light coat of a clear acrylic coating such as Krylon.

Asbestos. Many things in the home are made of asbestos. Because of its non-flammability, it is used for hot-pads, ironing-board covers, shingles and many other things. Asbestos ironing-board covers can be made to last longer by giving them an occasional washing in plain soap and water. Rinse and allow the cover to dry thoroughly before it is used for ironing. Mild scorches can be removed by adding a small amount of ordinary bleach to the rinse water.

Asbestos shingles will last almost forever, but their surface will need an occasional coat of paint. To save yourself a lot of grief, we suggest that you use a water-based latex paint. You can apply latex paint over damp asbestos shingles. To use a solvent-based paint, the asbestos must be absolutely dry. A more important reason for using the latex paint is that it allows the house to "breathe". That is, moisture behind the shingles can pass through, and not remain trapped where it can cause rot.

Whichever paint you use, be careful to clean the asbestos surface thoroughly first; remove dirt, soot, and matter that could prevent a good contact between paint and the asbestos surface. Two coats should be applied, whichever paint you use.

Asphalt tile. Tile made of asphalt will give many years of service if the surface is kept free of grit and no abrasive cleaners, oil polishes or polishing waxes are used. A monthly washing with mild warm water and soap suds is all that is needed. If you must wax, use only a self-polishing water-wax preparation. There are some special cleaners recommended by individual tile manufacturers.

Bathtub. When properly cared for, the surface of a porcelain bathtub will last indefinitely, but being over zealous with an abrasive cleaner will ruin the glazed porcelain. As the surface is worn by the cleaner, it becomes increasingly more difficult to clean, so more cleanser is used. It becomes a vicious circle. Warm soapy water, or plain washing soda is really the best. If you have a build-up of soap, a cloth soaked in kerosene will do the job. Just flush away the residue and the smell and soap will be gone.

Rust stains can be removed by rubbing them with a little lemon juice.

Brass. Brass is a tough alloy that is difficult to damage, but it discolors easily. Some brass is lacquered to preserve the finish. This surface should only be washed in warm water and mild soap. If any part of the lacquer is scratched off, the exposed brass will begin to take on a darker coloration. Use a commercial brass polish to brighten the exposed surface and apply a fresh coat of lacquer over it.

Uncoated brass surfaces can be preserved by using salt and hot vinegar. Common washing soda or trisodium phosphate mixed with water is often as effective. If the brass item can be placed in a pot, try boiling it in a water bath of trisodium phosphate. Whatever is used to do the cleaning, the brass surface should be flushed thoroughly after the washing. Dry and buff to a shine with a dry chamois. If a high shine is desired, use one of the commercial brass polishes.

Brick. Brick walls are made of unglazed brick, which has a rough surface. This surface can collect dirt until the original color of the brick almost vanishes. Usually a washing with warm water and trisodium phosphate (one ounce of trisodium per gallon) will do the trick. Stubborn stains that cannot be removed can be masked by first wetting the brick and then rubbing the surface with another piece of brick of the same color. (Figure 1-1.)

Brick can be damaged by vines. An ivy covered brick chimney is pretty, but the little plant fingers that attach the ivy to the surface can gradually erode the mortar. It's a long process, but one worth acting to prevent if you have a chimney covered with ivy. If the mortar is loose, it's best to remove the ivy.

A settling chimney can have little cracks, which of themselves are seldom dangerous. But, if water lodges in them and freezes, the expanding ice can do a lot of damage. Look for these cracks and patch them with a mortar mix before winter sets in. It's also a good idea to check the top of the chimney once a year where the liner and the bricks meet. The constant expansion and contraction that takes place as the chimney heats and cools can cause cracks that should be filled.

Glazed, or smooth brick is most often used for floor surfaces. Regular dry-mop dusting and a monthly washing with warm, sudsy water is all that is needed to keep them sharp. Watch for any gritty material on the surface; this can cause rapid wear and the loss of the glaze.

Cement. Cement floors should be protected by a coat of cement paint. This coating will not only make it difficult for dust to

Figure 1-1:   **Stubborn stains on brick can be hidden by rubbing a spare brick over the discolored area. Wet the two surfaces first.**

lodge in the pores, it will also help slow down surface wear. If the appearance is of little importance, but waterproofing is desired, you can apply a coating of water-glass. Sodium silicate, or water-glass, can be bought at most hardware stores, and should be mixed one quart of water-glass to four quarts of water. The floor should be clean and dry before the coating is applied. Three or four coatings will be needed and you should wait a day between each application.

Chromium. Household products finished in chromium have a high metallic luster with a bluish hue. Chromium won't rust, but often appears to rust because the base metal, to which it has been plated, rusts. Avoid getting any salts on a chromium surface; it will pit rapidly.

Coarse and caustic cleansers should never be used on chromium. A mild soap or detergent and warm water is all that is needed to protect the surface. Ordinary silver polish will brighten a long-neglected surface.

Copper. Copper weathers outdoors and oxidizes to a green color. Indoors, the green on water pipes and other functional copper items is not expecially harmful. Copper cooking vessels must be kept scrupulously clean; the copper oxide is toxic.

There are a number of commercial copper cleaners, but before you spend the money, try this simple formula: Mix equal parts of salt, flour, and vinegar together to form a paste and rub in on the dull copper. This should do the trick in all but the most stubborn cases. To preserve a copper luster on anything but cooking pots, apply a coat of paste wax or lacquer.

Fireplace. We've already discussed brick, but the inside surface of a fireplace can occasionally benefit from a cleaning. You will never get all of the carbon from the surface, but a thorough scrubbing with a strong mixture of warm water and trisodium phosphate will loosen a lot of the soot.

Keep the fireplace free from ashes (Figure 1-2). Although a bed of ashes makes it easier to start the next fire, these ashes can blow into the room and settle on everything, giving you a big cleaning job. If you discover loose mortar, replace it before you build another fire. Here's what to do:

1. Clean the crack carefully with trisodium phosphate or Soilax.
2. Dig out all loose mortar.
3. Mix Porock, or similar high temperature mortar, to a heavy consistency, and fill the crack.

Avoid spilling anything on the hot bricks. This can cause cracking.

The chimney should be inspected each spring and cleaned when needed. This is an ambitious job better handled by a professional with the right tools and brushes.

Floors. Floors are made of many different materials, but most can be treated with the same types of polish. However, the different types of polishes require different maintenance treatments. Floor polishes are made up of a coating substance to provide the finish and a carrier which makes it possible to spread or pour the polish. Coatings can be natural or synthetic wax, a chemical polymer or a combination of wax and polymers. The carriers are

Figure 1-2:   **Removing ashes from the fireplace won't do much to extend the life of the fireplace, but it will prevent loose ash from damaging furniture, rugs, walls, and clothing.**

made up either of solvents or water. As the polish is applied to the floor, the carrier evaporates, leaving the polishing agent on the surface. Read the label of commercial polishes to find out whether the carrier is water or a solvent.

How to clean floors polished with water-based, self-polishing liquids. Damp mop with warm water. If the water is too hot it will soften and cloud the finish. Scuffs and scratches can be removed by a damp mop with warm water and a light coat of polish to the scuffed area. A very light rubbing of grade 000 or 0000 steel wool, will lift black heel marks. The rubbed area will have to be re-waxed. Do not use steel wool on "no-wax" floors or on embossed vinyl asbestos. You can also use a good cleaning solution, such as Top Job.

How to clean floors polished with solvent-based, self-polishing liquids. Light soils can be lifted by damp mopping, but heavier scuffs must be rubbed with a warm, damp cloth. A gentle rubbing with 00 steel wool will lift heel marks and heavier scuffs. Recoat and polish the surface.

How to clean floors polished with buffable paste or liquid-based or solvent-based polishes. Light soils can be removed by buffing with a weighted brush. Then use a lamb's wool pad for a more satiny appearance. Heavier scuffs and stains can be handled by rubbing the surface with a cloth dampened in warm water. Number 00 steel wool can be used to lift black heel marks. Repolish and buff the area.

For best results, resiliant types of flooring such as linoleum, asphalt tile, rubber tile, vinyl asbestos, and vinyl sheet should be coated with a water-based polish. Solvent-based polishes can soften the surface and dramatically shorten the life of the floor.

Wood and cork floors should be protected by a solvent-based polish. Water and water-based polishes hasten the decomposition of wood and cork. To get the years of life built into wood and cork floors avoid any contact with water.

Hard surface floors such as those made of marble, terrazzo, ceramic and similar materials should not need a surface polish. However, if you do want to add more luster you can use either a solvent- or water-based polish. There are some silicone sealers that work well on these surfaces. These sealers are usually available where tile is sold.

Glass windows. Routine washing can be handled by simply using cool, clear water. Change the water as it becomes dirty. If, however, the windows are quite dirty, you might add a tablespoon of ammonia or vinegar to a quart of water to help break up heavy soils. If you're going to wash windows during a freezing day, add a half a cup of alcohol to each quart of water to prevent it from freezing.

Care should be exercised when using cleaners that contain alcohol, soda, ammonia or other alkaline constituents. These chemicals can damage surrounding surfaces such as paint and lacquer.

Use a chamois dampened in whatever cleaner you have selected, to wet and wipe the surface. A light buffing with a dry chamois or lint-free cloth completes the job. Whatever you do, don't buff a dirty window with a dry cloth; this will scratch the surface. And avoid the use of soap as a cleaning agent; no matter how much you rinse, you are bound to leave some soap film that will mar the finish. Soilax works very well and doesn't leave a soap film.

Gutters. Rain gutters should be cleaned at least twice a year, and more often if they accumulate a lot of debris from nearby trees. To make sure that you get your money's worth in gutter life, the inside surfaces should be treated every few years. Wood gutters should be treated with linseed oil; tin and galvanized metal gutters can be preserved with a coating of liquid roofing. Copper and aluminum gutters are best maintained by a coat of spar varnish every few years.

Leather. Leather loses its luster and begins to crack when it dries out. You can get extra life from leather by first gently washing the surface with a cloth dampened in warm soapsuds. After rinsing away the suds, apply a coating of neatsfoot oil while the leather is still damp (Figure 1-3). This oil will penetrate the pores of the leather and extend its life greatly. Important: For the care of leather clothing and shoes, see Chapter 5.

Mirrors. A mirror should be cleaned the same way as a glass window. But to make sure that you get all the use you can from a mirror, make sure that no water or glass cleaner gets behind the frame to the back surfacing. The reflecting surface can be permanently damaged.

Oilcloth. The life of oilcloth can be extended by observing these few hints. Never fold oilcloth when it is wet; it will crack along the fold lines. Don't leave it in the sun for long periods of time. Clean stains before they set, using only warm, sudsy water. Don't use gritty cleaners, alcohol or other solvent cleaners. And avoid laying hot pots on the surface.

Paint. Paint fades, and loses its surface over time. There is very little you can do to prevent this. But if you plan to wash a painted surface, you should select the cleaning methods that will clean best, yet not harm the paint. To begin with, you can't wash a whitewash or calcimine coating. Oil paints and the new synthetic-resin paints can be washed, but you should use only a mild soap and warm water. Abrasive and coarse cleaners will make the finish rough. In fact, if you plan to paint over a painted surface, it's a

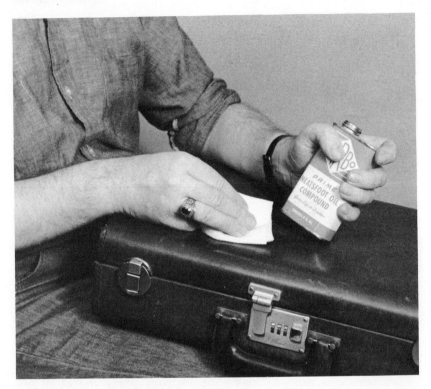

Figure 1-3: An application of neatsfoot oil will add years of life to leather. Apply a light coat to leather which has been dampened with water.

good idea to give the wall a good scrubbing with trisodium phosphate. This chemical, available in most hardware stores, will thoroughly clean a wall covered with flat paint and will remove the gloss from enamel paint. To repaint a high gloss wall, you should roughen the surface, and a treatment of trisodium will do the trick.

If paint peels regularly from the outside walls, the chances are that moisture is getting behind them and working its way through to loosen the paint. This means finding the source of water entry, or installing ventilation holes in the area where the paint is peeling. These vents, available at hardware stores, are round plug-like devices with tiny louvres and a screen to keep out bugs. A one-inch hole is drilled and they are simply pushed into place. They can mean the difference between a one-year and a five-year paint job.

Plastic. Many household products are made of plastic, or have some components of plastic. Each plastic is selected by the manufacturer for its special qualities; some are hard and brittle, others are soft and pliable. Each type of plastic requires different attention. Here are the major plastics used in household products and how to get extra years of life from them.

Acrylic is a fairly rigid type of plastic that is most often used for brush handles, jewelry boxes, kitchen bowls and other products where some abuse is expected. Most household chemicals will not affect acrylic, but these solvents will cause problems: alcohol, nail polish and polish remover, perfumes and similar compounds. Products made of acrylic will burn slowly. Never clean acrylic with anything abrasive. Scratchy cleaners and steel wool will put an end to the luster. Use mild soap and luke-warm water. Hot water can soften acrylic and may cause it to lose its molded shape.

Nylon is a plastic which can be boiled, banged, bent and subjected to most household solvents without being affected. Nylon is most often used for bowls, brushes, and ˏkitchenware. Even though it washes easily and can be put in a dishwasher, food stains should be wiped off before they set. As with most other plastics, you should not use abrasive cleaners and steel wool on the surfaces.

Phenolic is used to make the lustrous parts you often en-counter on irons, vacuum cleaners, cameras and other home items. It is hard, rigid and maintains a glistening surface with very little cleaning. Oils, alcohols, and most solvents have no affect on phenolic parts. The best cleaning procedure includes the use of only warm water and a mild soap. Don't use anything abrasive such as scouring powder or steel wool. Phenolic won't burn, but it will char. Keep phenolic parts away from high heat and an open flame.

Plexiglass is just a trade name for acrylic. See acrylic for details on this material.

Polyethylene is a plastic which can take a lot of abuse from both heat and cold. It is used to make the ice-cube forms for ice trays because it doesn't become brittle in the cold. It can take a lot of heat—even brief encounters with boiling water—but for longest life it should be used at temperatures below $150°$ F. Most household chemicals won't hurt polyethylene, but you should avoid touching it with cleaning fluids.

Polystyrene is a rigid plastic which can be subjected to freezing temperatures; hence its popularity for freezer containers.

Most household chemicals will not damage polystyrene, but nail polish and remover, cleaning fluids, and the oil from citrus fruits, will damage it. It should be washed in warm water and mild soap or detergent. Avoid the use of abrasives such as scouring powders and steel wool.

Rubber. We've already talked about the care of rubber floor materials, but there are other items in the home made of rubber that can be made to last a lot longer with some simple care. Rubber boots and overshoes should be kept away from heat, and stored in a cool dark place. Any fats, oils and acids that have been spilled on rubber surfaces should be flushed with lots of water right away.

Soiled rubber products can be cleaned by adding a tablespoon or two of ammonia to some sudsy water. Be sure to rinse completely.

Sinks. Sinks can be cleaned as we have described previously under the heading of bathtubs. However, one of the best ways to get long life from your sink is to make sure that nothing cracks the surface. If the surface is chipped down to the base metal, the metal will rust and stain. Sinks made of all ceramic materials or stainless steel will not have this problem.

Steel. A lot of steel is being used in kitchens these days. Sinks, drain boards, and trim can be ordered in steel. Stainless steel won't rust, but it will pit from contact with salt and acids. The acid from a lemon, if left sitting on stainless steel can do some damage. Most salt and acids can be removed by lightly rubbing with a very fine steel wool. There are cleaners on the market that work well. It may be necessary to try several to find the cleaner that will work best on your particular stainless steel sink.

Tempered steel is used for knives and other kitchen utensils. This metal will corrode and rust. Wash tools made of tempered steel immediately after use. Use a good scouring powder. If these tools are dried thoroughly, they will not get a chance to rust.

Tile. Glazed ceramic tile takes quite a beating, but it can easily be roughened by the repeated use of gritty cleansers. Once the glaze has been abraded, there is nothing you can do to get the finish back. Mop with mild cleaners, and use trisodium phosphate for the stubborn stains.

Unglazed tile can be cleaned with gritty powders, but don't use them too often; each application takes a little of the surface with it.

Never let water stand for any length of time on a ceramic tile floor; it will loosen the mortar used to hold the tiles in place.

Wallpaper. One of the practical reasons for using wallpaper is to extend the time between wall covering jobs. Painted walls usually require work more often than wallpaper. To make sure that you do get this benefit from your wallpaper, there are a few points to remember.

Most problems with wallpapers occur when they are being cleaned. Some wallpapers are not washable, and others that are supposed to be washable, run when being cleaned. So, the best advice we can give you to extend the life of your wallpaper is to test a spot in an inconspicuous area. Use as little water as possible, don't rub too hard and use the mildest cleaning agent you can get your hands on. In fact, first try to do the job with plain water before adding a cleaner to the water.

Wash only a small area at a time, working from the bottom of the wall to the ceiling. Overlap your strokes slightly, rinse with clear water if a cleaner is used and blot dry immediately with a clean cloth or paper towels. Avoid getting the paper too wet; this will not only cause the print to run, it will also loosen the glue.

Wallpapers that are definitely marked as being not washable should be cleaned only with the commercial cleaner made for this purpose. This is a doughy substance, available at hardware and paint stores. Smaller marks can often be removed with a soft eraser such as an art gum.

LUBRICATION IN THE HOME

Proper lubrication of things that move and rub against other things will greatly extend the life of the items. In other chapters, we discuss the more common things that need lubrication—your automobile, furnace, appliances and other obvious home products. But there are a number of other spots in your home that should be lubricated to insure extra years of life. By not lubricating some things, you can cause considerable wear in other items. For example, a caster on the leg of a heavy chair that is not lubricated will stick and drag, rather than roll over a rug. This can quickly damage the rug.

Here are a few rules to observe when lubricating household products:

1. Never overlubricate. Overlubrication can cause as much damage as underlubrication. If you are in doubt as to how much oil or grease is required, either use as little as possible, or contact the manufacturer of the product. Also, check to be sure that wear points are not lifetime lubricated and sealed at the factory.

2. Be sure that you use the right lubricant for the job. Using oil where grease is required will cause damage; lubricants aren't interchangeable.

3. Clean the surface to be lubricated before applying the lubrication. Any grit, dust and dirt on the surface will stick with the newly applied lubricant and hasten surface wear.

4. Don't wait for the squeaks before applying a lubricant. When something squeaks, it is wearing. Anticipate this by a periodic application of lubrication before the wear takes place.

Which lubricant? These are the most important lubricants for household use:

Silicone grease. Silicone grease is most often used to lubricate sliding wood parts and occasionally metal surfaces. It is available under a number of different brand names, as either a stick, or in spray cans. You can also buy tubes of silicone grease in radio parts supply houses.

Light oil. This thin oil is used for small appliances, and power tools driven by motors rated at 1/8 horsepower or less. This includes drills, fans, automatic can openers and similar equipment.

Heavy oil. This thicker oil is used to lubricate electric motors larger than 1/8 horsepower that are most often found on attic fans, furnace blowers, washers and dryers, oil burners, and larger power tools.

Liquid graphite. Made of a mixture of powdered graphite and oil, this lubricant is most often used on surfaces which face the weather: garage-door hinges, outdoor-furniture hinges, garden tools, and especially locks. This mixture will stain clothes; be careful.

Most of the things in the home that need oil can be lubricated about twice a year. Here are some of the major household items that should be lubricated:

Locks. Every type of lock can benefit from an application of graphite oil twice a year. Apply the graphite to the surface of the sliding bolt and work it in and out several times to spread the oil.

Powdered graphite blown into the key slot and worked in by the key, will keep the lock in top shape (Figure 1-4). WD-40 will also work well. Keeping the key slot lubricated is especially important if there are a number of people using different keys in the lock. When one key is used more frequently, it may cause the lock pins to wear to the point where a less frequently-used key may not open the lock. Good lubrication will prevent this wear.

Figure 1-4:   **An application of graphite to the moving parts of a lock once or twice a year will keep the lock from sticking.**

Power tools. Light household oil applied as recommended by the manufacturer will keep your tools humming for a long while. Seldom are more than two or three drops needed at each oil hole. (Figure 1-5.)

Hand tools. Tools that don't move can benefit from light oil on the surface occasionally to prevent rusting. Tools that move, such as pliers, should be cleaned and oiled about twice a year. Use light oil or silicone grease.

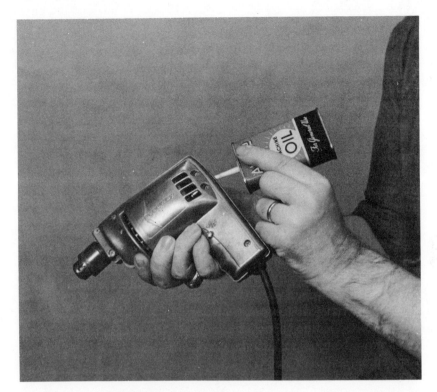

Figure 1-5: **Power tools should be lubricated in accordance with the manufacturer's instructions. Some require grease and others are to be oiled. Be sure you know which lubricant to use. If in doubt, check with the dealer who sold you the tool.**

Furnace blowers and pumps. Heavy oil is called for with this equipment. Two or three drops twice a year in the oil cups is usually all that is needed.

Faucets. A drop of light oil twice a year in the stem (the rod that connects the handle to the top works of the valve) will prevent wear and leaks.

Drawers. A light covering of silicone on the sliding surfaces will not only make drawers easier to use, but it will forestall the problems of a stuck drawer.

Hinges. It's almost a waste of time to apply oil to a hinge without first removing the pin. Once removed, the pin, and the inside surfaces of the hinge, should be cleaned. One or two drops of oil should then be applied to the pin and spread evenly over the entire surface.

On hinges from which the pin cannot be removed, apply a drop of oil at the top of the pin, and work the hinge back and forth to spread the oil evenly.

Double-hung windows. A light application of silicone, soap, or paraffin wax, twice a year to the window channels is all that is needed to make windows operate smoothly in all kinds of weather.

Casement windows. The cranking mechanism should be given one or two drops of oil twice a year, and the hinges should receive a drop at the same time. To prevent damage to the cranking mechanism, clean the surfaces of the metal frames to make sure that the windows close snugly.

Aluminum storm windows. Aluminum storm windows that contain both the glass and the screen can be made to operate effortlessly by a twice yearly application of silicone to the channels. A light spray or rubbing with a silicone stick is all that is needed.

For details on lubrication of household items not discussed, see the index.

Chapter 2

Home Furnishings:

How to select, use and maintain carpeting, drapes and furniture.

Getting the most for your money, and making your home furnishings last longer, begins with a careful purchase. Of course, all the use and maintenance tips we offer in this chapter will still be worthwhile if you have already bought your furnishings.

CARPET AND RUGS

A few years ago, if someone put a carpet in the kitchen, many people would have laughed. But today there are some good and practical reasons for putting carpeting here, and in other seemingly unusual places. In fact, there is hardly an area, inside or outside the home, that cannot benefit from some type of floor covering.

One of the best ways to make sure that your carpeting will wear well is first to make a careful study of materials available based on your needs, and the use and intended location of the carpet.

Usage. Your home is like a town with a number of streets. Some streets get more use than others and have to be repaired more often. A carpet in a family room will get much more wear than a carpet in a bedroom. Therefore, consider these points of usage when you select carpet:

Doors and furniture will, for the most part, determine where the wear will take place. Where there is heavy foot traffic, it is important to select a top quality carpet. You can't move doors to change the traffic, but you can occasionally rearrange the furniture to give other parts of the rug a share. To solve the traffic-at-the-door problem, you might want to use a small scatter rug right over the carpeting. Scatter rugs in front of a favorite chair will help keep the wear to a minimum, too. (Figure 2-1.)

Figure 2-1:   **Place a scatter rug in front of a favorite chair, and you will cut down on the wear of the rug.**

• On stair carpet, the edges wear a lot faster than the fabric on the treads and risers. Therefore, when the carpet is being installed, make sure to have about a foot of additional carpet folded in under one or two of the risers. This will never be noticed, but will allow you to shift the carpet up or down a few inches at a time to hide the wear that will show at the edge. Once flattened on a tread or riser, the wear is seldom obvious.

• A loose rug placed in a high traffic area will often be kicked and tripped over until the edge begins to curl. To prevent accidents and rug curling, simple use double-face tape between the rug backing and the floor. This tape is available in hardware stores.

• Exposure to direct sunlight can fade and damage the fibers of some fabrics. Try to have drapes, shades or blinds closed during periods of direct sunlight to prevent this problem.

• When some carpeting is exposed to dampness, or conditions of high humidity, mildew occurs. If you can't eliminate the dampness, you might try one of the indoor-outdoor fabrics which are usually made of synthetic materials not affected by moisture. If it is a problem of only humidity, proper ventilation can often clear up the situation. Keeping the windows open during dry periods will help.

Floor coverage. There are practical and esthetic reasons for the different ways of covering a floor with carpet. For example, a wall-to-wall installation not only has a luxurious look, it also can hide a problem floor. Consider these points before you decide how to carpet your room.

• Wall-to-wall will give your room a bigger look, muffle noises, and tie together a decorating scheme. It won't move and has no edges over which someone might trip. But it is expensive to install, and cannot be shifted to compensate for wear. It is also difficult and expensive to remove for outside professional cleaning. However, it is simple and inexpensive to clean wall-to-wall carpet yourself, with rental equipment and cleaners.

• A room-fit carpet has the look of wall-to-wall because it is cut to fit against the baseboard. But it is not tacked down, as is wall-to-wall. It is easy to lift for outside cleaning, and costs less to install. However, it cannot be moved to hide wear and it may be difficult to clean the floor around the edges. In smaller sizes with heavy traffic, it can shift slightly, leaving the floor exposed.

• Room-size rugs are cut in sizes roughly the same as standard rooms; 8' x 10', 9' x 12' etc. They are easy to install, can be repositioned to hide wear and stains, and are easily lifted for outside cleaning.

• Area rugs are smaller than room size rugs and are often used to supplement a room size rug in odd shaped areas. They are easy to move and lift for outside cleaning.

• Scatter rugs are usually made in sizes smaller than 4 x 6 feet and are seldom made of the same fabrics found in broadloomed carpet. They are easily shifted and cleaned, but can be dangerous if they do not have a non-skid backing. The double-face tape mentioned earlier can solve this problem.

Carpet problems. Some carpets can be tended with only an occasional vacuuming while others require almost constant attention. These problems are discussed in detail later under the headings of fibers and textures. The following points apply to all carpeting fabrics:

• Light colors show dust and dirt very quickly. If you select a light-colored carpet, be prepared to vacuum it frequently. This is not only an added chore, but the more frequent vacuuming will wear the fibers. If your home is heated by a hot-air system, light colors should be avoided. Dust and dirt particles will be deposited around the registers.

• Dark colors will show lighter things such as lint and hair.

• Carpet with an even texture will show dirt and lint more readily than will a rug of uneven texture; but uneven texture rugs are more difficult to clean. The extra cleaning can add to the wear problems.

• To solve these problems, if your decorating scheme will tolerate it, we suggest that you consider patterned rugs with two or more colors. "Pepper and salt" patterns will hide soils and they do not have to be vacuumed as often to maintain a good appearance.

Selecting the right fiber. Today, synthetic fibers predominate in the manufacture of carpeting. For example, nylon is used in almost half of the carpets manufactured in the United States. Not all carpet materials are the same; each has its advantages and disadvantages. Understand the qualities of each, and you will be on your way to getting extra years out of your floor covering purchases.

• Nylon has good resilience, and can seldom be completely crushed down by a chair leg. Its color fastness is excellent and it wears very well under heavy traffic.

Carpets woven from short, rather than long continuous fibers, can fuzz up under hard wear. Some nylon carpeting will produce static charges when the humidity is low. However, there are chemical sprays available to reduce this problem.

• Polyester is soft and luxurious in appearance, and has good colorfastness and wear resistance. However, it is not as resilient as nylon. Look for a deeper pile when you are considering this fiber to make sure that you get good resilience.

• Acrylic fiber is soft in appearance, has good resilience, colorfastness, and wear resistance. It is not affected by humidity and dampness, but it may fuzz and form "pills" when heavily used.

• Modacrylic is a fiber usually blended with acrylic in larger carpets to increase flame resistance. However, it is sometimes used alone in bathroom and scatter rugs. It has moderately good resiliency and fair to good wear resistance.

• Wool was, at one time, one of the main sources of fiber for carpet manufacture. Wool has a soft, pleasant appearance, excellent resilience, takes dyes well and has a good resistance to soil and wear. It is an excellent fiber, but the synthetics are now less expensive to produce.

• Polypropylene is used mostly in the manufacture of indoor-outdoor carpet and for commercial installations. It is not damaged by moisture, has good wear resistance, excellent resistance to water-based stains, and moderate resistance to oil-based stains. Its colorfast qualities are excellent. It does, however, have poor resilience.

• Rayon is a relatively inexpensive fiber that is used mostly in bathroom and scatter rugs. It has poor resilience and only fair resistance to wear and stains.

• Cotton, the only other natural fiber used regularly in rug manufacture, has poor resilience, but good to excellent colorfastness. It has fair soil resistance, but the fact that cotton is easily laundered makes the fiber a good choice for small scatter and area rugs.

• Blended fibers are often used to take advantage of the important characteristics of several materials. All carpets made of blended material must show the percentage by weight of each fiber used. A number of different blends exist, but if any fiber comprises **less than 20% of the total, it is unlikely to affect the carpet quality.**

Evaluating carpet construction. Different constructions have different life expectancies. The weave itself, and the amount of cleaning necessary will determine the life you get from a particular piece of carpet.

- A tufted rug is one in which loops or tufts of yarn are pulled through the backing and often held in place with an adhesive backing. Most carpets made in the United States are tufted. Look for the number of tufts per square inch. The more tufts, the better the quality and the longer the carpet will last.
- Woven carpet is made by intertwining the yarns to produce a single fabric. A well-made woven carpet can be counted on for its durability.
- Needlepunched carpet is made by punching a fiber sheet and interlocking loose fibers. This results in a dense, feltlike carpet which is modestly priced and sold primarily for outdoor or kitchen use. When used in the kitchen, it should be cleaned regularly to prevent a build-up of soil which may be difficult to remove.

Choosing the right texture. In addition to different ways of making carpet, the manufacturing process can produce a number of different surface textures. Understand the benefits and drawbacks of each, and you can help make your carpet last much longer.

- Level loop pile is of uniform height, wears well and hides footprints. However, it shows dust and lint readily. Because it is easy to vacuum, regular maintenance will contribute very little to wear.
- Cut pile carpet is made by cutting the yarn loops so that they stand up straight from the backing. It looks quite luxurious, but it shows dirt and lint readily. It shows shading (the "shadows" you see when the texture is flattened in different directions). Cut pile carpet is relatively easy to clean.
- Level-tip shear is a carpet which is level, with some yarn loops cut and some uncut. It shows dirt readily, but hides footprints better than cut pile. It is not difficult to vacuum.
- Multilevel loop is a fabric in which loops of different levels appear on the surface. Footprints do not show easily and dust and dirt is less visible. However, it takes more effort to clean than a level pile carpet.

- Random shear is similar to multilevel loop, but the higher loops are cut. This texture hides footprints and dirt well, but is more difficult to clean.
- Sculptured carpets are sheared to make designs on the surface. Dirt, dust and footprints are readily hidden, but it is more difficult to vacuum than a level pile.
- Shag rugs are deeply piled loops or cut loops that are widely spaced and have a rough, tumbled look. Shag hides footprints, dust, and dirt, but can be very difficult to vacuum. To prevent life-shortening fraying, use a special shag attachment on your vacuum. There are even shag rakes to help keep these rugs in shape.
- Twist rugs are made by tightly twisting the yarn and heat setting it to increase the resilience and durability. Twist wears well, hides footprints and dirt, and is not difficult to clean.

Carpet paddings. The use of a high-quality pad under the carpet can double the carpet life by absorbing crushing loads on the rug surface. The pad can make an inexpensive carpet last much longer than it would with no pad. It also makes the carpet feel better underfoot, and insulates against heat, cold, and noise. Some carpets are made with a permanently mounted backing. The sponge or latex foam-rubber backing should be at least one-quarter inch thick.

- The use of a pad protects the rug backing from wear on a rough or uneven floor.
- Furniture legs and other heavy objects kept on a rug are less likely to leave permanent depressions when a padding is used.

Caring for your carpet. Regular care and tending to special problems quickly will help extend the life of your carpet. A daily once-over with a manual carpet sweeper or a vacuum cleaner will prevent dust and grit from working its way deeply into the carpet. Pay particular attention to areas where there is heavy traffic. A thorough cleaning weekly with a vacuum cleaner will keep the rug looking new and help it last much longer. The following tips were suggested by the Carpet and Rug Institute, and represent a sensible way to get the most out of this expensive investment.

- Small diameter furniture legs will crush carpet pile. Shifting the furniture frequently only a few inches will prevent this. (Figure 2-2.)

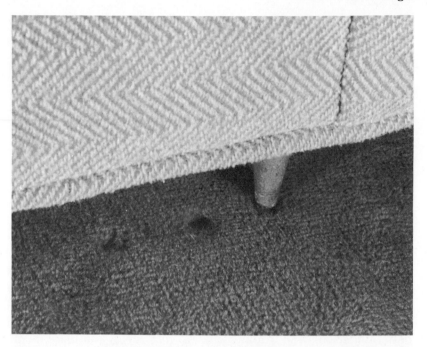

Figure 2-2:   **Holes like these can be made when a furniture leg is placed directly on the carpet. Use large coasters to prevent this problem.**

• If yarn has been badly depressed, it is often possible to bring it back to life by holding a steam iron about six inches over the mark (Figure 2-3) moistening the fibers with the steam and working the tufts back and forth with either your fingers or the edge of a large coin.

• Use furniture glides (cups) to spread out the weight of small diameter legs on rug surfaces. Even when this is done, the furniture should be moved a few inches regularly.

• When a tuft of yarn appears loose, or higher than surrounding tufts, never pull on it, you may remove an entire row of yarn. Cut the extended tuft level with the surrounding tufts. (Figure 2-4.)

• When using the vacuum, move it slowly over the carpet surface to allow the suction to remove embedded soil particles. For best results, move the vacuum in different directions, but the final strokes should be in one direction to give a uniform surface.

Figure 2-3: Hold a steam iron about six inches above a depression caused by a furniture leg and release some steam. Work the steamed fibers with a large coin to eliminate the hole.

• Placing small mats at doorways leading to rooms with carpet will help collect much of the foot dirt before it reaches the rug.

• Indoor-outdoor carpet should receive much the same attention as conventional carpet. However, much surface litter is easily removed by using a broom or deck brush. If you wash this kind of carpet, be sure that it is thoroughly dry before you attempt to vacuum it.

• Clean your bath mats in a washing machine. Use only a mild detergent and then tumble-dry. Hang the rug on a line and face an electric fan on it to finish the drying. Never try to iron these rugs.

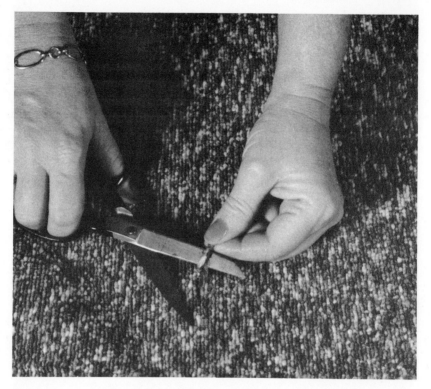

Figure 2-4:   **Never tug on a loose strand of a rug. Cut it off flush with the surface of the carpet.**

• Small burns can be removed by carefully clipping away the burned area. Don't cut too deeply in level pile carpet.

• Prompt attention will prevent most spills from leaving a permanent stain. Try the following steps:

1. Remove the spill immediately; solids with a spoon and liquids with cloth or paper towels.
2. Use a small amount of drycleaning fluid. Pat the soiled area gently, working from the edge of the stain toward the center. Never use the carbon tetrachloride, gasoline or lighter fluid.
3. Dampen the spot with a solution made of one teaspoon of mild powdered detergent and a cup of water.
4. Make a pad of paper toweling about one-half inch thick and place it under a weight over the spot. When the pad is

soaked replace it with another until the spot is dry. This should take about 6 hours.

5. Brush the dry surface to restore the fluffiness.

CURTAINS AND DRAPERIES

Whether you buy ready-made draperies and curtains or make your own, the choice of fabric is perhaps the one most important factor in extending their life. Each fabric has its advantages and disadvantages.

Selecting fabrics. Read the labels carefully, and examine the weave. A simple understanding of the following points will help you make the right choice.

• Sheer fabrics should be chosen with care. These materials are made with a loose weave, so the yarn used should have strong fibers for the best wearing qualities. Polyester is considered the best for marquisette and ninon fabrics. In addition to having high physical strength, polyester has good resistance to the fading effects of sunlight and pollutants.

• Batiste and voile fabric, made with polyester blended with cotton or rayon, has good wearing qualities and is easy to care for. These blends are best for opacity.

• Glass fiber is most often used in heavier fabrics with an open-weave appearance. This material has very good resistance to sunlight and atmospheric pollutants.

• In general, cotton, acrylic and glass fibers give the best service in curtains and draperies when they are the only fiber in the fabric. Blends of the following types have been most satisfactory: cotton and rayon, cotton and polyester, rayon and polyester, and rayon and acetate. Cotton, acrylic, polyester and glass fibers are more resistant to sunlight fading than are rayon and acetate.

• The durable-press fabrics are easy to care for. The most satisfactory finishes in this category are blends of polyester with cotton or rayon.

• Not all dyes and coloring are equally resistant to sunlight fading. Undyed fabrics or very light shades of color may be the better choice in areas of intense sunlight; and color change will be less noticeable. If darker fabrics are a must for the decorating scheme, you might consider regular rotation, moving draperies from windows of high sunlight exposure to windows with lesser exposure. This way, the color change will be gradual, and not dramatically noticeable.

• Linings in draperies will help protect the main fabric against sunlight fading and appreciably lengthen the useful life of good draperies or curtains.

• Unless the fabric has been preshrunk, or is made of a fiber that will not shrink, you can have shrinkage problems when there is high humidity and during cleaning. When fabrics are woven, the fibers are stretched. Moisture makes the fiber relax and results in a shrunken curtain or drape.

Some fabrics can be restretched, but the best solution is to make sure that there is a little extra fabric in the hem that can be let out after the shrinkage has taken place.

Cleaning curtains and draperies. If you have lost the label or cleaning instructions which accompanied your curtains or draperies, these hints can help prolong their life.

• Fabrics of 100% rayon and blends of rayon with cotton or acetate should be dry-cleaned to prevent shrinking.

• Glass-fiber fabrics should never be machine washed or dry-cleaned. Handwash this fabric gently in mild detergent.

• Linen can be machine washed and tumble dried, or dry cleaned.

• Cotton can be machine washed and tumble dried, or dry cleaned.

• Wool can be laundered, but cold water and very mild detergents must be used. Dry cleaning is safer.

• Acetate can be home laundered, but should never be wrung out or twisted, Dry cleaning is preferable.

• Modacrylics can be machine washed in warm water and tumble dried at low temperatures.

• Nylon can be machine washed and tumble dried at low temperatures.

• Polyester can be machine washed and tumble dried.

• Rayon can be machine washed and tumble dried. Do not twist or wring out.

FURNITURE

To make sure that your furniture investment is protected, we suggest that you heed the following precautions:

General care of all furniture. Whether upholstered or plain wood, these tips will help to extend the life of your furniture.

• Avoid placing uneven stress on the legs. A table that rocks back and forth because of an uneven floor is not only a bother, but starts loosening the other legs. Often, something as simple as a thumbtack in the bottom of a table leg will be enough to set it straight. Leaning back on two legs of a chair is the fastest way to ruin it. The weight and uneven stress will loosen every joint in the chair.

• Whether casual furniture is delivered unassembled or is supplied assembled, it is often possible to do a little tightening occasionally to keep it in shape. Breakfast room furniture, dinettes, and similar pieces will loosen in time. Don't wait until the wobble becomes intolerable before you tighten bolts. Serious damage can be done by this time. The same idea applies to all other furniture, but it is often difficult or impossible to tighten the pieces. Wooden furniture can often be disassembled and reglued, but this is a major repair project beyond the scope of this book.

• Furniture placed in hot rooms will dry out. The finish will soil and the glue will dry out. Direct sunlight will cause upholstered fabrics and wood surfaces to change color.

• Dampness can result in mildew in some fabrics and cause the wood fibers to expand. A dehumidifier in a damp room will prevent these problems. A coat of wax on wood surfaces will prevent moisture from getting into the wood fibers.

Upholstered furniture. These tips refer primarily to the fabrics of upholstered furniture. Some upholstered furniture has exposed wood surfaces. Care of these surfaces is the same as that given furniture of all-wood construction, and is discussed in the next section.

• Zippers are used in upholstered furniture to assure a good fit and to simplify the replacement of the inner cushion. Do not remove the covers for cleaning; they may shrink and become impossible to replace.

- Cushions should be vacuumed once a week.
- Do not brush upholstery fabric with a stiff brush.
- If the cushions are reversible, turn them each time you vacuum.
  - Fluff-up pillows filled with down or other loose material.

Cleaning upholstered furniture. There are ways of removing just about every kind of stain. The list is long, and beyond the scope of this book. But a very good booklet is available at many furniture stores; *How to Care for Your Upholstered Furniture.* It is published by the National Association of Furniture Manufacturers, Inc. If you will follow these precautions, you will have very few stain problems and will help extend the life of your upholstered furniture.

- Clean up spills immediately. Once set, anything spilled on upholstery will be hard to remove, and may stain permanently.
- If you are attempting to clean a stain, pre-test the cleaner you plan to use on an unexposed area of the upholstery. The cleaner may add to the problem, shrink the fabric or cause the color to bleed. When testing for shrinkage, allow the fabric to dry at least one hour before assuming it is safe to go ahead with the exposed stain.
- If you find that your cleaning agent causes the color to bleed, you might try adding two tablespoons of white vinegar to the bucket of foam, and to the rinse water.
- The best procedure to remove a stain is to begin by lifting the staining material. Then use a solvent which is compatible with the fabric and then a water based detergent. To help the consumer decide which method to use, a joint committee of a number of home-furnishing associations have adopted this code appearing on the label.

W— Use water-based cleaning agents or foam. Cleaning by professional furniture service is recommended.

S— Only mild, pure, water-free, dry-cleaning solvents may be used for cleaning this fabric. Cleaning by a professional furniture service is recommended.

W-S— Water-based cleaning agents and foam may be used for cleaning. This fabric may also be cleaned with mild water-free solvents.

X— This fabric should be vacuumed or brushed lightly to remove soil. Do not use foam or liquid cleaning agents of any kind.

- When using water, it should be lukewarm. Hot water can set a stain permanently.
- Never soak a fabric, whether you are using water or solvents. Dry the surface by blotting, not rubbing. Be sure to dry thoroughly fabrics cleaned with solvents. Some cushion stuffing materials can be damaged by solvents.
- Water should not be used on rayon fabrics. This synthetic fiber can shrink.
- When cleaning a spot, use a clean sponge and work from the outside of the stain to the center. This will prevent enlarging the stain.
- Dry the treated stain area quickly. Blot up excess liquid, and try using a hair dryer at low temperature or an electric fan over the damp surface. Covering the spot with pure talcum powder will help absorb the moisture (Figure 2-5). The talcum is vacuumed off after the surface has dried.

Wood Furniture. Wood furniture and the wood surfaces of upholstered furniture should be cared for regularly to insure long life and beauty.

- Frequent dusting—two to three times a week—with a clean, lint-free, absorbent cloth will not only keep the furniture appearance up, it will also extend its life.
- Washing wood surfaces once a year will prevent soils from permanently damaging the finish. Work quickly, use lukewarm water and only mild soap or detergent. Wash, rinse and dry small areas at one time; don't work on a whole chair at once. Be sure not to let water penetrate wood joints. The joints will swell, and the glue will be loosened.
- Always clean the surface before applying a fresh coat of wax or polish. Old wax can be easily removed by using either mineral spirits or a synthetic turpentine. Regular turpentine leaves a sticky residue and a lingering odor. As with water washing, work a small area at a time; clean, dry, and move on.

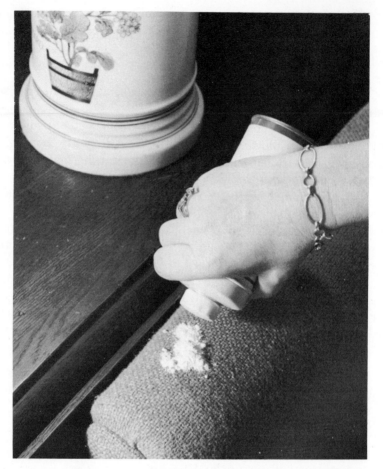

Figure 2-5:   **To speed up the drying of a dampened spot, apply a small pile of talcum powder. Vacuum the powder after the spot has dried.**

• Liquid spills should be removed immediately by blotting with a dry cloth or paper towel.

• If you are trying a new polish or cleaner, pre-test it on an area that is not exposed to view.

• Nail polish remover is one of the most harmful household liquids. It will soften and lift finishes very quickly. It can be a mistake to wipe this spill immediately. It is often better to let the spill evaporate first. Then rub the area with a very fine grade of steel wool. Apply wax after this, and you may save the surface.

• Even though a surface is described as burn resistant, the wood below the surface can be charred. You may not see this, but it will ultimately result in the surface lifting and causing an ugly bulge.

• Cleaning and polishing should be done only with a clean, lint-free cloth. If you use old clothing, make sure the buttons have been removed and avoid using a seamed cloth on the surface of the wood.

• When dusting, waxing, or cleaning surfaces, always work in the direction of the wood grain.

Preserving wood surface finishes. All wood finishes cannot be treated alike. Follow these tips to maintain the beauty of all wood surfaces.

• High gloss finishes can be kept up with either paste wax or liquid polish. Use a thin coat and lots of rubbing. Follow the specific instructions on the polish you plan to use.

• Satin-gloss finishes should be cleaned with polishes that do not contain silicone. Silicone will add a luster that is unwanted in soft finishes. If repeated waxings produce a glossy finish, remove the wax build-up with mineral spirits and recoat with fresh polish.

• Low-gloss finishes should be preserved by using polishes that clean but do not increase the luster. If wax is used, apply it sparingly and in small areas. Buff immediately until the surface is hard and dry.

• Oil finishes should be washed occasionally with mineral spirits and refinished with boiled linseed oil. Rub this finish vigorously until it is free of oil. Never use regular linseed oil; it is sticky and leaves a tacky residue.

Safety note: Never leave oil soaked rags lying around. Spontaneous combustion can cause serious fires. Dampen used rags with water and dispose of them immediately.

• Paint finishes should be washed with a mild soap or detergent and water solution. Never flush the wood surface with water; use only a dampened cloth.

Laminated plastic surfaces. Even though laminated surfaces are rugged and very stain resistant, they must be cared for occasionally.

• Don't place hot pots directly on these surfaces.
• Don't slice food directly on the plastic surface; use a cutting board. (Figure 2-6).

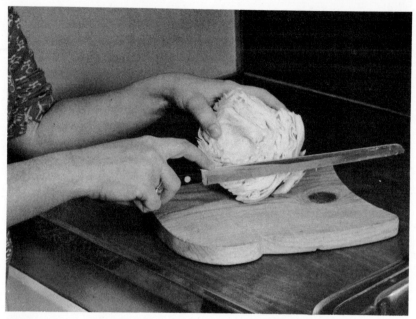

Figure 2-6:   **Formica is tough, but all cutting should be done on a cutting board.**

• Wash with a mild soap or detergent solution only.
• Liquid-cleaner waxes are recommended to protect the surface of laminated plastic surfaces.

Leather surfaces. Except for dusting regularly, the only maintenance that should be used with leather is an occasional application of hard wax. Never use liquid wax on leather surfaces.

Marble surfaces. Marble needs careful handling to prevent chipping, and its surface can be kept looking new and fresh for many years if you follow these tips.

• Wash only with lukewarm water and clean cloths. Use a mild detergent no more than twice a year to remove resistant dirt. Scrub with fiber brush and dry quickly to prevent streaking.

- A light paste wax will protect marble surfaces, but never wax white marble. In time the wax will yellow, leaving the white marble with a yellow haze.

Chapter 3

Appliances:

How to get the best possible return on major household investments.

For virtually no cost and only a few minutes of your time, you can do simple things that will save you, for example, the $300 or $400 needed to replace a washer or dryer that might have lasted another 3 or 4 years. You can, with nothing more than a little knowledge, make sure that your expensive garbage disposal unit will not only last many times longer, but will greatly reduce future plumbing problems.

It isn't necessary to have any mechanical or electrical skills to make sure that your appliances give you the full measure of the service you paid for. Follow the special tips and suggestions found in these pages and you will be assured of getting every year of life built into your appliance by the manufacturer.

Before we discuss individual appliances, there are a few things applicable to all appliances that you should know.

LUBRICATION

Some appliances require periodic lubrication; others are lifetime lubricated, or use systems which do not require the addition of oil or grease. Make sure you know which appliances need lubrication, how much to use, and when to do it. If you have lost the *Use and Care* manual that accompanied the appliance, it is often possible to get an extra copy from the store that sold you the unit. If the dealer has none to spare, don't hesitate about writing to the manufacturer for another copy.

Lack of lubrication, or improper lubrication results in friction: friction causes heat and wear and a shortening of the life of an appliance. Here is what happens when you place a few drops of oil in the bearing of an appliance:

- The drop of oil reduces friction
- It conducts heat away from working surfaces
- It seals out contamination
- It prevents rust and corrosion
- It adds years to the life of the unit

ELECTRICAL CONSIDERATIONS

Many of the problems encountered by service technicians are located in the electrical portions of the equipment. But these problems could have been avoided with a little care. Here are a few tips to follow with all your electrical appliances:

Avoid excessive flexing of the electrical cord. These cords are made of stranded wire to permit flexing, but every piece of metal has its breaking point. Most cord breakage takes place either right next to the plug, or where the cord enters the appliance. Keep this in mind when you use electrical appliances. Loop cords loosely.

Don't pull out plugs by the wire. Pull the plug out by holding the plug, not the wire. Pulling the wire will result in the wire pulling off the plug terminals or breaking.

Clean the plug prongs occasionally. The brass prongs of electrical plugs should be brightened up when they get dark. Do this with either very fine sandpaper, emery cloth, or nonsoaped steel wool. The dirt that collects on these prongs can add resistance to the line and reduce the efficiency of the appliance.

Don't overload circuits. Plugging a toaster, hair dryer and other appliances into the same circuit at the same time can cause problems for the units and even blow fuses. It is better to use different circuits for different appliances. Above all, don't think you are expanding your electrical service by using plug-in multiple outlets or extension cords. You may get more outlets, but there is still the same amount of electricity available in the line. This is a definite fire hazard. (Figure 3-1.)

Turn appliances off after you have finished using them. When you leave an appliance on after you have finished using it,

Figure 3-1:   The octopus: A danger in many ways. It can blow fuses, start fires, and spread wires to trip people. Never try to add to the capacity of an outlet with such an arrangement.

you will not only use more expensive energy, you will wear the unit out sooner. Appliances, regardless of how well you take care of them, do have a finite life, and the more you use them, the sooner they will wear out.

Unplug major appliances during a power failure. When the power company restores service after a failure, it usually comes on slowly; you've seen the lights come on dimly at first, then continue to brighten until the full power is on. Major appliances, such as freezers and refrigerators must operate at full-line voltage. If they go on with the returning low voltage, they may suffer serious damage. Wait until you know the power is on—and will stay on. Then re-plug the appliances.

Use grounded plugs and outlets. Most newer homes are built with 3-wire grounded circuits for maximum safety. If your home uses a two-wire system, it is possible to buy adaptor plugs for this added safety. When you install them, be sure to connect the wire to the screw on the outlet plate. Without this connection, you are no better off than you would be with the old two-wire outlet.

Don't poke around inside electrical equipment. There are lethal voltages inside every plug-in appliance. And, believe it or not, people have gotten serious shocks from an unplugged television set. TV components called capacitors store high voltages that can be released even when the plug is out. The electrical tips we offer on individual appliances do not involve touching any of the critical electrical circuitry. Follow these tips, and you will have a longer lasting appliances—and no surprise shocks!

Here are the hints and tips that will help you prolong the useful life of many of the appliances—both large and small—that you own and use each day. To make this section as easy to use as possible, the appliances are listed in alphabetical order.

AIR CONDITIONER

One of the best ways to insure long life and economical operation from your air conditioner is to locate it correctly, and to keep cold air from leaking to the outside. Always remember that cold air is heavier than hot air. If you have an air conditioner on the first floor, and leave the cellar door open, the cold, dry air from your air conditioner will spill down the stairs. Your air conditioner will work twice as hard in such a case. Follow these location tips and you will get the most out of your air conditioner:

• Install the air conditioner on the shady side of the house. Whether the unit is a window model or an externally operated central cooling system, it will work better and last longer if the sun never touches it.

• Make sure that door saddles and moldings fit snugly. Small cracks are impossible to eliminate, but simple weather stripping will prevent cool air leakage, and reduce the time the unit must run to do its job properly.

• Don't place any obstructions in front of the unit. When the fan has to work harder to push air past an obstruction, it will wear that much faster.

• Whenever possible, prevent direct sunlight from entering an air-conditioned room. Radiant energy from the sun will force the air conditioner to work harder. Pull the blinds or shades; close the curtains or shutters.

• Don't wait until the room gets too uncomfortable to turn the unit on. The air conditioner then has to work hard to "catch up" on the accumulated heat. Anticipating the need, and turning the unit on early, will not only be better for the air conditioner, but will keep you more comfortable.

• Make sure windows are closed, and that spaces around window-mounted units are sealed. Some air conditioners are supplied with special sealing strips. If yours doesn't have these baffles, or if they don't fit tightly, cover the cracks with tape.

• When the air conditioner is in use, close all windows and doors. It is often tempting to leave a door open to another room to cool it down, also. But air conditioners can do only so much work. An open door gives it too much, and will reduce the life of the unit.

• Make sure the air conditioner is the right size for the room. The store selling you the air conditioner can give you this information before you buy it. If you find that you have a unit which is too small for a particular room, it is best to move it to a smaller room, and buy another properly sized unit to handle the large room.

• Be sure that the wiring is adequate. Check the capacity of the circuit, and the current rating of the air conditioner. If they are close, you may only be able to use one appliance on the line. It is often wise to have a separate line installed to serve only the air conditioner. It's not that expensive, and will leave you with outlets that can be used for other electrical equipment without fear of overloading.

Routine care of an air conditioner can insure top performance and long life. These simple steps can be taken by anyone:

• Clean the filter regularly. The filter is usually found right behind the grille that faces into the room. Grilles are removed easily, but each manufacturer has his own system. Either check the manual, or examine the grille to determine what kind of catches are used. These grilles are designed to be removed, so don't be afraid of prying a little. When the grille has been removed, you will find a sheet of porous material, usually foam rubber, through which the air is filtered. Either wash this in warm sudsy water, or vacuum it thoroughly. (Figure 3-2.) A clogged filter means lower efficiency, less comfort, greater wear on the motor, and a shortened life. It is impossible to give an accurate timetable for cleaning the filter. You

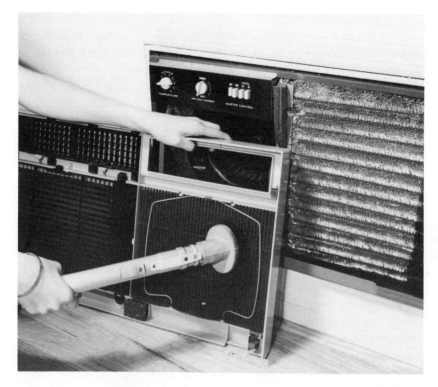

Figure 3-2:   **To make sure your air conditioner lasts longer, keep the filter clean. Inspect the filter monthly during the cooling season and clean as required.**

should examine the filter at least monthly during the cooling season to see how fast it gets dirty.

• Vacuum the outer grille. The grille can be a source of dust and dirt which will find its way to the filter. By vacuuming the grille everytime the rug is cleaned, you will save the number of times that the filter must be cleaned or replaced.

• If the evaporator (the coils seen in the back of the unit) freeze up, turn the unit off. It could be that the outside air is too cool, usually 70° or below, or that there is a problem in the unit. It's best to call a service man to handle such a problem.

• Inspect the condenser coils, as seen through the grille on the back of the air conditioner. This system will resemble the radiator in a car: it will have a lot of metal fins surrounding metal tubing. If this is dirty, or clogged with dust, remove the entire unit from the case and clean the condenser thoroughly. It is seldom possible to clean the condenser through the grille, and you may bend the metal so that it will interfere with proper operation.

• If the instructions call for lubrication, follow the manufacturer's recommendations.

BLENDERS

By taking the following precautions, you can make sure that you get longer life from your blender.

• Follow the manufacturer's recommendations on what to chop and what not to chop.

• When you are chopping hard things, or blending thick liquids, it is best to start slowly and gradually increase the speed.

• Don't overfill the container with hard-to-blend material. It is better to blend smaller quantities several times.

• Wash, rinse, and dry immediately after use. When moisture is left in the bowl, corrosion will set in and jam the blending assembly. When this step has been neglected, the motor will often smoke, then burn out completely.

• Don't poke into the blades with anything while the blades are turning.

• Avoid getting gritty material in the container. This can ruin the gasket which seals the shaft and cause leaks later on.

• Never use this appliance while it is in a puddle of water.

COFFEE PERCOLATORS

The electric percolator is one of the most popular appliances. It is also one of the most abused. Following these instructions will not only ensure that you get the most service from the pot, but also that you get the best coffee.

• Make sure that the water temperature is between $175°$ and $195°$F. The appliance can be checked by an appliance serviceman, or with a cooking thermometer. When the temperature is below $175°$, the coffee will be watery; above $195°$, it will be bitter.

• Accumulated lime deposits from tap water will spoil the taste of coffee, and shorten the life of the pot. You can remove the lime deposits by heating water to which you have added a few tablespoons of baking soda. This will also get rid of the coffee-stain deposits that contribute to a bad cup of coffee.

• Never start your percolator with warm or hot water. This shortens the perk time and gives a weak cup of coffee. Start with water that is about room temperature.

• Be sure not to let any coffee grinds get down the stem of the pot. There is a little pump at the bottom of the pot that brings the water up the stem and sprays it over the grounds in the coffee basket. Grounds in this pump will clog the mechanism, give you a weak cup of coffee, and add to an early failure of the pot.

• Coffee oils build up in the well of the percolator. After a while, the accumulated oils form an insulating barrier which causes the thermostat to open prematurely and stop the perk cycle before the coffee is properly brewed. The result is weak coffee, and causes people to use more grounds than should be necessary. Clean the pot often.

• Be careful not to submerge a non-immersible coffee pot. Water will ruin the heating system.

• Loose handles should be tightened as soon as they are noticed. Water can enter the screw holes and cause problems with the threads, so that the handle will loosen enough to break. Many coffee pot handles are only held on by simple screws. Just tighten the screw until the handle is firmly back in place.

GARBAGE COMPACTORS

The motor and mechanism of a garbage compactor develops tremendous forces. It is important to follow the manufacturer's instructions carefully when using this appliance. These tips will also help keep it running in top shape.

• Make sure that the unit is level. Many compactors have adjustable leveling legs.

• Use only plastic-lined paper bags, and follow the individual manufacturer's instructions for bag installation. If ordinary paper bags are used, liquid will be squeezed from the garbage, through the bag, and into the compactor. Trouble can start very quickly when this happens.

• Even though most compactors are key operated, it is possible for children to turn them on and be injured. Keep the keys out of the reach of children.

• Cleanliness contributes to long life. Make sure that both the inside and outside of your compactor is kept clean. The drawer should be removed regularly and completely cleaned. While the drawer is out, remove and clean the ram cover and the wiper blade. Warm water and a good detergent are all that are needed to do an acceptable job.

• Keep the disinfectant aerosol spray nozzle clean. This can be done with the tip of an ordinary toothpick.

DEHUMIDIFIERS

The refrigerant type of dehumidifier is very much like an air conditioner, except that the entire unit is located within a room, and there is no external vent of warm air. These units become most effective at higher temperatures. However, even under the best of conditions, it is seldom possible to bring a room down to more than 40% or 50% relative humidity. However, this can mean the difference between sweltering and considerable comfort. Follow these hints for the best results and longer life:

• A dehumidifier operating properly will save you lots of problems, other than humidity. When there is excess moisture in the air, metals rust, foods become moldy, cold water pipes sweat and drip all over, wood swells and causes sticking doors and drawers.

• Be sure that the unit you buy is sized to the room in which it will be used. Check the manufacturer's suggestion as to room size.

• Place the dehumidifier so that the end grilles are at least 6 inches away from any obstructions. Only air that passes through the unit will be dehumidified.

• Close all doors and windows in the area to be dehumidified.

• If the evaporator freezes up, it might be that there is poor air circulation. Try moving it to another location. If this fails, you will have to call a serviceman.

• The collected water should be emptied regularly. Some dehumidifiers have automatic level sensors which will shut the motor off before the water begins to spill over, but others must be checked visually.

• The collected water is pure and usable in steam irons and other appliances requiring distilled water. You can pour it through a coffee filter to remove any dust and grit that fell into the reservoir during operation.

• Every few weeks, scrub the inside of the water container with a mild detergent to prevent the growth of mold, mildew, or bacteria.

DISHWASHER

Dishwashers can be portable or permanently installed. These comments apply to both types of machines.

• Be sure that the dishwasher is operated from a level position. This is especially important to check with portable units. Use a glass of water for a rough approximation of level.

• The minerals found in hard water can damage a dishwasher and prevent best washing action. If the content is high, it is wise to install a water softener ahead of the dishwasher.

• Water temperature should be kept between 140° and 160°F. If the temperature is not within this range, it is best to call a plumber to handle the adjustments on your water heater.

• Make an occasional empty run, using two cups of vinegar instead of detergent. This will prevent lime deposits from building up.

• Don't overload the dishwasher, but don't run it half full either. The same amount of water is used, regardless of the number of dishes stacked inside.

• Make sure the cups, bowls, pots and glasses are positioned so that they can drain.

• Use the detergent recommended by the manufacturer, and in exactly the specified amounts. Too much sudsing will clog the pump and reduce the washing action. Excessive suds will also prevent the force of the water from performing the proper scrubbing action on dish surfaces.

• Be sure to scrape carefully all items to be placed in the dish-washer. Small bones and other foods can jam the pump and possibly burn out the motor.

GARBAGE DISPOSAL

A sink-drain mounted garbage disposal unit is a very efficient grinder. Food scraps are flushed through the unit, and ground so finely that they will flow into the sewer along with the waste water. Never put anything like glass, rubber or foil into a garbage disposal unit.

• The disposal must never be run without first having turned on the water. The unit is cold-water lubricated. Cold water congeals grease so that it can be ground up and flushed away. Hot water would keep the grease in a liquid state in which it would enter the sewer line and congeal to cause a clogged pipe.

• The flow of water should be about two gallons per minute. You can get a feel for this rate of water flow by setting your faucet to fill a half-gallon milk jug in about 15 seconds. It is a good idea to remember the position of the faucet so you can turn the handle to this spot every time you use the disposal.

• If your sink empties into a septic tank, instead of a city sewer system, don't grind such things as clam shells, cigarettes and other inorganic wastes.

• Let the cold water run for at least 20 seconds after the last bit of waste has been ground up. This insures that all waste material will be flushed through your drain line.

• Don't overload the disposal unit. Feed in the waste only as fast as it can be handled without straining. If a jam occurs, wait for about five minutes before turning it on again. The motor must be allowed to cool down. If your disposal has an automatic re-set, you can start it by simply turning the switch; others will have to be reactivated by using the manual re-set button.

• Some disposals have automatic or manual reversal systems to solve a jam problem. Follow each individual manufacturer's instructions when using a disposal in reverse. Never put the jam-breaking tool, supplied by some manufacturers, in the disposal unless the power is off. And never, ever, put your fingers down inside!

• Do not use drain cleaning chemicals in the disposal. These agents can corrode and severely damage a drain-line disposal unit.

CLOTHES DRYER—ELECTRIC

An electric clothes dryer is essentially a heating system, a drum to hold and tumble the wet clothes and a system to circulate and vent the warm moist air. When treated carefully, a good electric clothes dryer should last many years. Follow these hints to get the most from this handy appliance.

• Before placing clothing in the dryer, be sure to empty all pockets. Small objects will damage the surface of the drum, and long thin things, such as pins, will poke through the holes and damage the heating element.

• Clean the lint filter after every use. Each lint filter is different, but most are simply wire screens and the collected lint can be "peeled" off very quickly. (Figure 3-3.)

• The interior of the dryer should be vacuumed about twice a year. Remove the power cord, and take off the cover on the back of the machine. This accumulated lint can cause a fire.

• The dryer should be level. Check this with a spirit level, or measure the distance from the top to the floor at the four corners. Any difference should be corrected so the dryer stands perfectly level. This will not only make the dryer run more quietly, it will add considerable life to the machine.

• The warm, moist air should be vented to the outside. This can be done with plastic tubes specially made for this purpose. Exhausting the moist air in the same room will raise the humidity, cause rusting of the dryer and other metal parts in the room, and lengthen the time needed to dry clothes. It is also possible to blow lint back into the machine when there is no outside vent.

• The dryer should be mounted as close to the outside venting port as possible. The vent duct should be short and direct. Avoid any bends or twists in the ducting. Long, turning ducts slow air flow and make the machine work harder.

• Do not exhaust the dryer into a chimney. Lint will collect in the flue and possibly cause a fire.

• When the vent has a little self-closing trap door, spend a few minutes once a month to clean the accumulated lint from it. As the

Figure 3-3:   **Always remove the lint from the filter of a clothes dryer after each use.**

lint builds up, the door will no longer close tightly when the machine has stopped. With the door open, cold outside air can flow in—and small animals will try to climb in for a warm retreat from the outside cold.

• Be sure that there is sufficient air entering the room in which the dryer is being used. An air starved dryer is a very inefficient and hard-working appliance.

CLOTHES DRYER—GAS

Everything we have said about the electric dryer applies to the gas dryer, except that the heat to do the work is produced by a gas flame, rather than an electrical heating unit. The only thing we can say about a gas dryer is, be careful when moving it. It is usually connected to the gas source by a flexible metal hose. This hose is designed to move, but it will definitely not take a lot of flexing.

When you move the dryer from the wall for its internal vacuuming, be very careful not to kink the hose, or put a heavy strain on it. Above all, if you smell gas, shut the dryer off immediately, open all the windows, and call the gas company.

HUMIDIFIERS

When there is too little moisture in the air you can have a number of problems; houseplants wilt, wood shrinks causing squeaks, leather dries out, wood furniture becomes unglued, static electricity is generated and makes dust stick to everything and your nose and eyes feel dry and uncomfortable.

When the air is dry, you will feel cooler than you would if the room contained more moisture at the same temperature. A humidifier can help you feel more comfortable at a lower temperature.

However, a humidifier should be used with care. If you put too much moisutre in the air it can cause exterior paint to peel, and window sills and frames to rot. It will also make your house more appetizing to termites.

• To get a feel for the right conditions under which to run your humidifier, first fill a dry glass with ice water. After it stands for a few minutes, little droplets of water will collect on the outside of the glass if there is enough moisture in the air.

• Avoid putting hard water in your humidifier. If you must use water with a high mineral content, clean the unit often.

• If hard water is used, it is possible to remove mineral deposits from the pad by removing it, and soaking it in vinegar, or one of the commercially prepared solutions designed for the job.

• Make sure that the reservoirs are always full. Under very dry conditions, it is possible for a room humidifier to use 4 to 5 gallons of water a day in an ordinary sized home.

• Make sure that the outer screen is kept clean. A dusty screen will prevent moisture from being properly distributed. Vacuum or thoroughly brush this screen as conditions demand.

ELECTRIC IRONS

There are two kinds of electric irons—the dry iron and the steam iron. Steam irons can also be used as dry irons.

• Clean the soleplate frequently to keep it free from stains. (Figure 3-4.) Use a mild household detergent or baking soda on aluminum, and a damp, soapy scouring pad on steel plates. After cleaning and rinsing, wipe the soleplate dry, select a low temperature and iron first over waxpaper and then over a dry cloth. Never use anything but a damp cloth or sponge on a nonstick soleplate. The nonstick feature is the result of a special coating applied to the soleplate. This coating can be scratched by scouring powders and other abrasive cleaners.

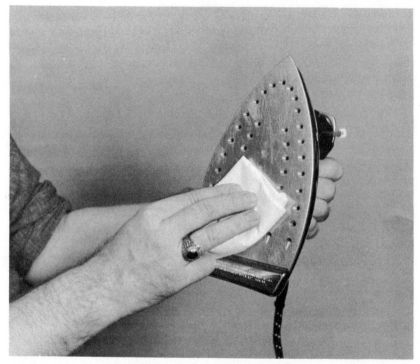

Figure 3-4:   **Remove starch from the soleplate of an iron with a coarse cloth, paper, or very fine steel wool. Scratches can be removed by a light rubbing of very fine emery cloth.**

• Don't use too much starch, or overheat the iron when working with synthetics. You will end up with a very sticky soleplate.

• Slight scratches on the soleplate will not harm fabric, but deep scratches and burrs will. Metal burrs can be removed by a light rubbing with either steel wool or very fine emery cloth.

• Use only soft (low mineral content) water in a steam iron. Minerals from hard water will clog the steam ports and cause streaking. Never use water treated with a chemical softener; it contains particles that can clog the ports.

• Demineralized water will often froth and spit when it is heated to a boiling point. This problem can be avoided by underfilling the iron slightly.

• Periodically rinse the tank and fill with fresh water. Leaving water in the tank after use, and just filling it up as needed is an invitation to an early repair problem.

• Distilled water is best for the steam iron, but you can also use clean rain water, or the water collected from a dehumidifier and from defrosted refrigerators. It is a good idea to filter this water through something like a paper coffee filter to remove any dust and grit that may have fallen. If you want to save rain water, or water from a dehumidifier, put it in a glass or plastic bottle and add a teaspoon of chorine bleach (Clorox) to each quart to prevent growth of bacteria.

• Keep the hot soleplate away from the electric cord.

• Keep the iron in the standing position (not flat on the soleplate) when it is not in use. Air dissipates the heat more quickly, and prevents the overheating that can damage the electrical element if the iron is left flat on the board. There are metal stands for this purpose, that conduct away the heat, but allow the user to leave the iron in the safer flat position.

ELECTRIC CAN OPENERS

With a little care, electric can openers will do their job for a long time.

• The round cutting wheel on a can opener should be removed occasionally. Dirt and grease accumulate on the shaft and cause the wheel to turn more slowly, putting a strain on the motor. A dirty wheel can also be a health hazard. The wheel is held on by a screw and is easily removed. (Figure 3-5.) Be sure to replace the spring when the wheel is put back on.

• The shaft on which the cutting wheel is mounted should be lubricated occasionally with a very light application of vegetable oil.

• Clean the teeth on the wheel that grips and turns the can. Clogged wheels are inefficient and will make the motor work longer and harder.

Figure 3-5:   **Clean the cutting wheel and related parts of a can opener regularly. Food particles are easily trapped and can be quite dangerous. Simply remove the screw holding the cutting wheel, and the entire assembly will come off. A light application of vegetable oil will keep the wheel lubricated.**

• Be careful not to let a can bind the opener to the point where the motor is forced to a stop. This can quickly burn out the motor.

• If the can opener has a knife-sharpening attachment, sharpen knives by lightly pressing the blade against the sharpening wheels and drawing the knife, handle first, toward you. If you press unevenly, you will damage the knife and the sharpener.

FOOD MIXERS

Food mixers come in a number of different syles, but basically there are two major types: those with attached bowls and the hand-held mixer that can be used with any bowl. Some mixers with bowls can be removed for hand-held operation.

• Be especially careful not to let things like spoons, knives— and fingers—get into the moving blades. In addition to damaging the blades, such a jam-up can damage or ruin the motor.

• Don't bend the blades; they are designed to mesh in a very precise way. It is possible that the grinding of the blades will put metal particles in whatever you are mixing.

• Don't try to mix very stiff materials. Mixing bread dough with a conventional mixer is asking for trouble. There are special attachments called dough hooks especially made for this purpose.

• When mixing heavy materials, start slowly, and gradually increase the speed, rather than turning the mixer on full speed right away.

PROBE-CONTROLLED COOKING APPLIANCES

Many of the newer electric frying pans, dutch ovens, and other cooking appliances have the temperature control unit in a removable probe. Wash the pan, as you would any other immersible electric appliance. Follow these instructions to get the most out of the temperature-controlling probe itself.

• Make sure that the probe is never immersed in water. If the plastic surface becomes grimy, wipe it with a damp cloth or sponge.

• Keep the metal surface of the probe clean by wiping it lightly with steel wool, or one of the plastic scouring pads. (Figure 3-6.) A probe with an accumulation of grease will become inaccurate and can deposit grease in the sensing well in the base of the pan.

ELECTRIC TYPEWRITER

These cautions apply, in general, to all typewriters. An electric typewriter is more prone to trouble simply because there are more things that can go wrong if the machine is not properly cared for.

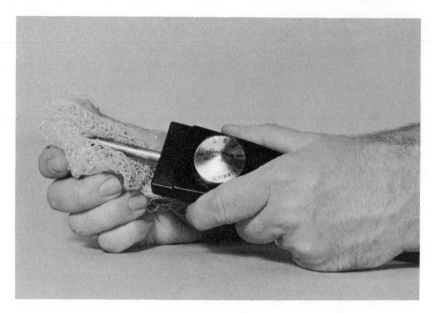

**Figure 3-6:   Clean the surface of the probe after each use. Use a plastic
pad or light steel wool.**

• Above all, keep erasure crumbs out of the works. Little
pieces of paper and eraser rubber will find their way to all of the
critical parts and make life miserable for you and the machine.

• Do not lubricate a typewriter unless the specifications call
for it. Many typewriters are permanently lubricated. An oily
typewriter not only collects erasures—if you erase—but it also gums
up very quickly from dust in the air.

• Keep the type faces clean with an occasional brushing with
an old toothbrush and alcohol or benzene. (Figure 3-7.)

• The platen, or roller should be removed twice a year and
cleaned with a mild ammonia based detergent. While the platen is
out, clean the small feed rollers that bear on the platen with the
same solution. Don't let this liquid run into the machine.

• It is often possible to blow out accumulated dust in a
typewriter by attaching the hose of a vacuum cleaner to the blowing
port and placing the nozzle under the machine. Be careful not to
bend any of the delicate mechanisms with the nozzle.

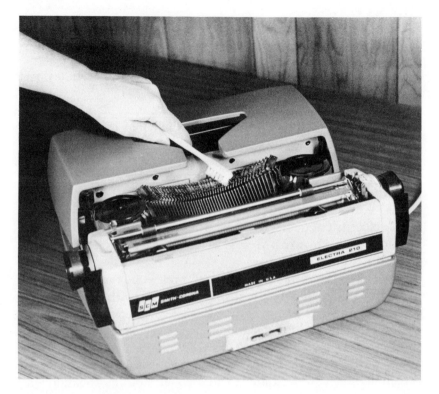

Figure 3-7: Use a toothbrush and alcohol to clean type faces. While you're at it, blow out accumulated lint and eraser particles.

ELECTRIC RANGES AND OVENS

The modern electric range has, in addition to the basic heating units, controls for accurate temperature regulation and timers of one sort or another.

• Avoid dripping food on heated cooking elements. If a spill occurs, allow the heating coil to cool before it is wiped clean with a damp cloth or sponge.

• Even though the heating elements are designed for safety, they can be damaged if hot pots are dropped on them, or if they are dropped when being removed for cleaning.

• All ovens have vents. A clogged vent will prevent moisture from leaving the oven. Oven walls will sweat and this will cause problems for some of the self-cleaning models.

• Do not use the stove to heat a room. There simply isn't enough heat available.

• Don't place pots taken from the heating elements on the porcelain surfaces of the stove. The porcelain may crack.

Self-cleaning ovens.

• The self-cleaning oven is not an incinerator, so don't expect to burn off large amounts of waste material.

• When the oven is cleaning itself, make sure that the door is tightly closed, and do not open the oven during the cleaning period. Admitting air while the oven is at its highest temperature could cause an explosion.

• Here's how to determine if your self-cleaning oven is working. When the oven walls are covered with a soft brown residue, nothing is happening; a dark brown condition indicates that the heat is insufficient to complete the job; a loose grey ash shows that everything is working OK.

• Continuous-cleaning ovens have a catalyst right in the porcelain that causes stains to lighten at normal cooking temperatures. However, continuous-cleaning ovens will not handle spillovers and spatters.

• To clean spillovers in a continuous-cleaning oven, first wipe the cooled-down oven with a nylon or other lint-free cloth dampened in plain tap water. Then blot the walls dry and run the oven at 400°F for an hour. This will also help the oven to catch up on stubborn stains.

• If you neglect spillovers, they will become hard and brittle at normal cooking temperatures. Don't try to remove them by scraping with a sharp instrument like a knife. Simply tap them lightly with the back of a large wooden spoon, and they should shatter and fall off the walls.

• Commercial cleaners should not be used on the surfaces of continuous-cleaning ovens. Use a stiff nylon brush or a dampened sponge. Scouring powders should never be used.

• Silicone sprays should be avoided. This chemical can clog the pores of the oven wall and prevent the catalyst from working.

Microwave ovens.

Metal containers should never be used in a microwave oven and the oven should always have something in it when it is being used. The energy generated by the magnetron must be absorbed by something.

• Above all, don't tinker with the oven. The door has a safety switch which shuts down the microwave generating system when it is opened. If this is damaged and the oven is opened during operation, it is possible to receive severe burns in a very short time.

• The door of the oven is sealed with a special electronic "weatherstripping" which prevents the microwave energy from escaping. Be careful not to damage this seal.

GAS OVENS AND STOVES

The gas stove and oven combination is a very efficient appliance, but unless cared for, this efficiency can deteriorate rapidly. Follow these steps and you will be rewarded with good meals, a long-lasting range and minimum gas bills.

• Avoid spilling food on the burners. If food spills, it will clog the burner openings and reduce the amount of gas that will be available to do the cooking. Clean these spills immediately.

• Burner heads can be removed for cleaning. Scrub them in warm soap and water. Do not use steel wool or other materials that may break off and clog the holes. (Figure 3-8.)

• Keep dust from collecting at any of the burner air intakes. This will alter the amount of air mixing with the gas and reduce heating efficiency.

• Locate the stove away from windows. Pilot lights can be blown out, and curtains can be blown over an open flame.

• If your oven shows condensation (water droplets on the walls) during pre-heating, leave the door open for the first few minutes of this stage. This will drive out the moisture.

• Never clean a hot porcelain surface with a wet sponge. The temperature change can cause cracks.

• Avoid the use of harsh, abrasive cleaning agents, coarse steel wool or sharp tools when cleaning porcelain surfaces. Oven cleaners should never be used on external surfaces.

Figure 3-8:   **Keep gas range burner heads clean by scrubbing them in warm water and soap or detergent. Make sure they are dry before reinstalling them in the stove.**

   • Acid spills, such as citrus-fruit juices, should be wiped up immediately.
   • Stay ahead of the spatters in the oven. Clean them with oven cleansers, or with brush and detergent before they become a heavy crust.
   • Avoid using any aerosol spray products near a stove when it is being used. The aerosol propellant can produce a corrosive deposit when it contacts an open flame.

• A light coating of baby oil will do wonders for the chrome trim on a stove. It prevents corrosion and staining.

• To make oven cleaning a lot easier, let a few tablespoons of ammonia stand in the oven overnight before cleaning.

• Each oven has a temperature sensing element. This metal, tube-like device is located at the top of the oven and it should be gently cleaned with a soapless steel wool pad. Oven cleaners should not be sprayed over this bulb. You can protect it by covering it with aluminum foil when cleaners are being used.

• The broiler should be cleaned after each use. To make this job easier, you might try covering the broiler pan with aluminum foil, then disposing of it and the accumulated grease after each meal.

• Opening and closing the oven during pre-heating and cooking can cause problems. In addition to the rapid loss of heat, the thermal changes can cause cracking of oven finishes.

• Don't crowd a lot of utensils in the oven. Try to keep each vessel 1 to 1 1/2 inches apart and away from the walls.

• Never cover the bottom of the oven completely with foil. This will prevent air circulation and cause an uneven heating.

REFRIGERATORS

The refrigerator is probably one of the most hard-working appliances in the home. It has to work hard to keep foods cool, or frozen; it takes the physical abuse of being opened and closed many times a day; and when opened, it must work harder to get the temperature back to where is was before. Even so, with a little care, a modern refrigerator will last a long time if you observe these hints:

• Cold air is heavier than hot air. When the refrigerator door is opened, the cold air will literally spill out. Planning where to keep things in a refrigerator will allow you to get to what you want without having to leave the door open too long.

• Pick a cool place for your refrigerator. When it is in the sun, or near a radiator, it will have to work harder, and wear out faster.

• Be sure that there is at least a few inches of space around your refrigerator. There must be enough space for air to circulate to carry away the heat from the compressor and the coils.

• Keep the floor under the refrigerator free of litter and dust. The coils of the refrigerator should be vacuumed frequently because the dust acts as an insulator and makes the unit work harder. You can get at the coils (tubes with thin metal fins attached) usually by taking off a front panel under the front door. On older models, you might have to get at the coils from the rear.

• The door seal is very important. If the seal is damaged, cold air will leak out of the box, and make the compressor work harder than it should. Look for nicks in the door gasket, or bent and dented metal or plastic where the gasket meets the box.

• The average refrigerator is designed to have its compressor system in operation between 55% and 65% of the time at a room temperature of 70°F. An increase in room temperature, or excessive opening and closing will dramatically alter this pattern. If cooling the room, or limiting the opening and closing of the door does not change an excessive on-and-off pattern, you should call a serviceman.

• Don't try to hasten the defrosting process by chipping at ice with a sharp tool. You can easily pick a hole through the thin aluminum and lose all of the refrigerant.

• If you notice water vapor condensing on the walls of your box, it is probably being caused by moisture from warm, moist foods. To prevent this, cover the foods before they are placed in the unit.

FREEZERS

Some freezers are vertical and look just like a refrigerator. Others are horizontal, and open from the top like a storage trunk. Because cold air is heavier than warm air, the cold from a vertical type of unit will spill out when it is opened. The chest type freezer prevents this from happening by having its door at the very top of the cold chamber. However, the door to a horizontal freezer should not be left open more than necessary. The normal heat exchange from cold and hot air will make the compressor work overtime.

• Make sure that the unit is level. Use a carpenter's level to check. Most freezers have self-leveling legs, but if yours doesn't, use thin strips of cardboard, linoleum or metal to shim up a low side.

• Be sure that the door gasket fits tightly. Look for dents in the metal or plastic body, nicks, rips, and tears in the gasket itself.

These nicks in the gasket can often be repaired with a flexible-drying glue.

- Keep the freezer in a cool spot. Sunlight and nearby radiators will make the freezer work harder.

- To prevent excessive opening and closing, plan your daily or weekly food withdrawals carefully. Move the food from the freezer to the refrigerator to hold for early use.

- Keep all grilles free of dust. Air must circulate to the compressor and the condensing coils to insure trouble-free and efficient operation.

TOASTERS

The toaster is simply a heating element and timer built inside a cabinet. Pop-up toasters will give long service with very little attention if a few precautions are kept in mind:

- As toast is made and taken from the toaster, crumbs fall inside the appliance. After a while there can be quite a pile of crumbs in what appears to be a very clean toaster. These crumbs must be removed—*from the bottom* (Figure 3-9). Do not turn the toaster upside down to shake the crumbs out. You will get some of the crumbs out, but you will also deposit a lot of dry bread between the heating coils and the mica insulation. This can not only shorten the life of the element, but it can also cause a fire.

- Never stick anything inside the toaster, whether the plug is in or out. If the plug is in, you stand a good chance of being shocked; if the plug is out, you might ruin the heating element. If it is absolutely necessary to reach in the toaster, be sure the plug is out and use a good light to see what you are doing. Avoid touching any of the heating elements. Be very gentle.

- Don't place the toaster in such a way that someone could trip over the cord. Toasters are usually put on a table only at mealtime. Therefore, there is seldom a permanent installation, and electrical cords are found draped from outlet to table. Be sure these cords are out of the way.

VACUUM CLEANERS

Vacuum cleaners come in various styles—cannister, upright, or tank. No matter what they look like from the outside, they all work the same and can benefit from these long-life tips:

Figure 3-9: **Empty your toaster of crumbs regularly. Never turn the toaster over and dump out; open the clean-out hatch on the bottom.**

• Make sure that the hose and nozzles are clear (Figure 3-10). Dust and small items can collect in the tube and restrict the flow of air and the dirt being picked up. This is not only inefficient, but extra work for the motor.

• Don't wait too long to empty the bag or other dust container. A clogged dust bag will also make the motor work a lot harder. Air drawn into the vacuum is used to cool the motor. A full bag cuts down on the air to cool the motor.

• It is a good idea to empty the bag when it is about 2/3 full. This still leaves air flow and will make sure that the motor will not overheat.

• Be sure that all connections are tight. Any loose fittings will reduce the suction of the unit; both you and the vacuum will have to work longer and harder to pick up the dust.

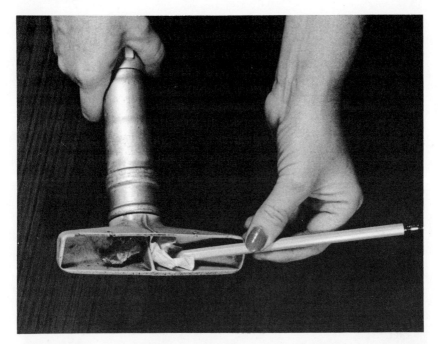

Figure 3-10: **Your vacuum will have to work overtime if the heads and tubes are left clogged. Inspect these parts after each use.**

• A quick way to check the efficiency of your vacuum is to put your hand in the air leaving the venting port. This air temperature should be between $20°$ and $25°$ warmer than room temperature. If it is higher, the chances are that the bag is too full, or that there is an obstruction in the hose of one of the fittings.

• It is best to use the exact replacement dust bags for your individual machine.

AUTOMATIC CLOTHES WASHERS

Automatic clothes washers come in many styles and models. These tips can be applied to lengthen the life of any model you may own:

• The washer should be installed close to hot water (about $145°$ is needed). Washers are connected to the hot and cold water by lengths of rubber hose and these hoses should be as short as possible.

• If the washer is draining into a house sewer line, it should feed a drain line or stand pipe that is at least 32" above the floor. Machines have drain hoses formed into a hook that can be hung over an adjoining sink. Make sure that the hose isn't knocked off the sink; you will have a room full of water.

• Avoid keeping the machine in a very cold area. Cold will cause the lubricants in the machine to thicken, and make the motor work harder. If the machine is allowed to stand in a freezing area, residual water may freeze and cause serious damage.

• It is important to close the hot and cold water valves when the machine is not in use (Figure 3-11). If the valves are left open, the hose will be under constant pressure, and it is quite possible that one will rupture when you least expect it.

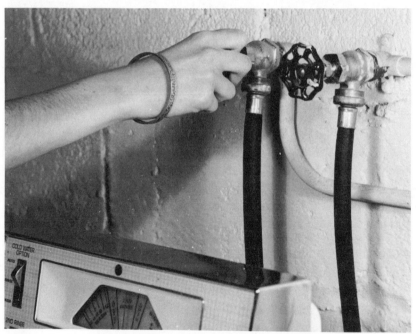

Figure 3-11:   **Turn off the water supply to your washing machine after you have finished using it. This takes the pressure off the hoses which otherwise may break after a few years use.**

• Follow the manufacturer's instructions concerning detergents. Excessive suds will not only give you a poor wash, but they will cause problems for the pump.

• Place the clothing so that it is evenly distributed in the cleaning basket. An uneven load will cause the machine to wobble, and this can wear out the bearings very quickly. It can also cause the machine to "creep" across the room. This pressure might be all that is needed to split a weakened hose.

• If water filters are part of your machine, clean them as suggested by the individual manufacturer.

• Never use cleaning solvents such as benzene in the machine.

• Remove everything from pockets before putting the clothes in the machine.

• Avoid holding any bleach water in the machine for longer than 30 minutes.

• If your machine is equipped with bleach and fabric softener receptacles, pour a quart or two of hot water through the opening every few weeks to eliminate any build-up. Automatic soap dispensers should also be cleaned frequently.

DENTAL WATER PICK

Convenience is important in locating this appliance. Place it so that tugging on the plastic tubing won't cause it to tip or fall from a shelf.

• Never let water freeze in the unit. Even after the tank has been pumped dry, there is often enough water in the pump to make a freeze harmful.

• Salt, dentrifices, and other chemicals should never be used in a water pick.

• Avoid kinking the tubing. This can put an undue strain on the pump and possibly spring a leak in the tubing itself.

AUTOMATIC TURNTABLE

Record players can be individual units, with cable connections to a separate amplifier or radio, or they can be units which are built into home entertainment combinations and complete sound centers. These tips apply, regardless of where the turntable is found.

• Be sure that there is adequate space for operation. Some turntables have rather elaborate arms and rods which are quite sensitive to shock.

- The turntable must be level when it is operating.
- Never let the stylus drop on a record or the turntable. The tip of the stylus can be damaged which, in turn, will damage all records played in the future. It is also possible to damage the cartridge in which the needle is mounted.
- If a dust cover is supplied, use it when the record player is not in use. Dust will collect in the motor, and on the stylus—both are places where considerable damage can be done.
- The drive motor should be inspected periodically and the dust vacuumed out. When you turn the player over to get at the motor, make sure that the tone arm and the changing mechanism are secure and will not flop free. Never rest the inverted unit on the tone arm or changing mechanism.
- When manufacturer's instructions specify, lubricate the motor with the recommended lubricant.
- Use the correct stylus for the record being played.

BATTERY-OPERATED RADIOS AND TAPE RECORDERS

Small portable radios and inexpensive cassette tape recorders often cost more to repair than their original purchase price. But, with a little care, these appliances should give years of adequate service.

- Be sure that batteries don't leak in equipment. There are leakproof batteries available, but if you plan to let the unit sit without using it for more than a month or two, it is a good idea to remove the batteries.
- Some units have a battery condition meter. Check the batteries each time you use the radio or recorder. You will know when the batteries are beginning to wear down, and you can have replacements ready.
- Tape recorders all operate on the same principle, but the steps which must be taken to run those made by different manufacturers differ widely. Be sure you know the sequence in which to run your recorder.
- Be sure that the batteries are placed in the proper position, + to + and — to —.
- Don't touch the recording and playback heads on a tape recorder with anything but a lint-free cloth moistened in a solution of isopropyl alcohol. This cleaning should be done as dust and oxide from the tape is seen building up.

- Keep the recorder away from magnets and magnetic fields.
- Keep battery-operated equipment away from heat and out of direct sunlight. This equipment should never be left in an auto glove compartment; temperatures can get very high in a closed car.
- Plastic cases can be cleaned with a damp cloth or sponge. Any water allowed to enter this equipment will be very harmful.

STEREO SYSTEMS

Some stereo systems are complete; that is the speakers and all components are in one cabinet. Others are available as components: radio, amplifier, turntable, speakers, and tape unit. These tips apply to all arrangements of stero equipment.

- The receiver or amplifier should be installed in a ventilated area. If the unit is allowed to get too warm, the useful life can be drastically shortened. Modern transistorized equipment is less likely to produce a lot of heat, but there is still a need for adequate ventilation.
- Long wire connections to remote speakers should be avoided.

- Avoid turning on an amplifier with no speaker connected. In certain types of circuitry, this could cause severe damage to transformers and other internal components. There are units internally protected against this problem, but unless you are certain that your unit has this feature, be sure to connect all the speakers before plugging in the amplifier.
- An outside antenna should have adequate lightning protection. There are different kinds of lightning protectors made for the ribbon and coaxial types of cable. Know which you have before you buy. They are not interchangeable. Then follow the manufacturer's instructions carefully when installing the protector.
- All units should be grounded. A look at your equipment will show you either wires or terminals marked "ground". Use a single length of wire, at least number 14 in size, to connect the equipment together. Then the wire should be firmly connected to an outside ground rod, or a *cold* water pipe. This grounding will not only protect your equipment from damage and yourself from shock, but it will also go a long way toward reducing problems of hum.
- If you are buying speakers that are not included as part of the stereo system, make sure that the speaker impedance matches

the impedance of the amplifier. Impedance is an electrical measurement that is stated in ohms. For example, if speakers are rated at 4 ohms, your amplifier output must match this figure.

• Don't overdrive the speakers. Modern stereo amplifiers have a lot of power, and some of today's music can drive a speaker to the point where the cone can be torn. If it hurts your ears, it's too loud—for you, your neighbors, and probably for your speaker.

TELEVISION SETS

Whether it's portable, or a huge console color set, your television can have its life extended by following these simple hints.

• Be sure the set is placed in a well-ventilated area. Don't stack books, magazines and other things around or on it; the circulation of air to the inside could be limited.

• When you wash the cabinet, use only a damp cloth.

• Never poke around inside the cabinet. Even unplugged, there are lethal voltages stored in capacitors in the set that could electrocute you.

• If you happen to drop your set, it is wise to have a serviceman look it over before you use it, even though it may still be working. This is more a safety precaution than anything else. A loosened wire can shock you or cause a fire.

• If an outside antenna is used, be sure to install the proper lightning arrester. There are different types for the ribbon and coaxial lines.

• Don't turn the set on and off rapidly in a short period of time.

• Never stand a drink on the top of the set. If spilled, it can ruin the set.

ELECTRIC FANS

Electric fans are available in all sizes and types. They all work the same and can benefit from these hints:

• Avoid bending any of the blades. This will result in an imbalance which will shorten the life of the fan.

• Face the fan into an open space. Any restriction of the air flow will make the fan work harder and shorten the life of the motor.

• Keep dust out of the motor housing. When you see it collecting, either vacuum it, or wipe it away with a dry dust cloth.

• Straighten all grille dents before the fan is started. If the blade hits a dented grille, it can cause damage.

ELECTRIC SEWING MACHINES

Whether a portable, or deluxe console model, you can extend the life of any sewing machine by observing these tips.

• Never let lint collect in any part of the machine. Thread moving through the mechanism deposits lint until there is a clogging build-up. Clean this lint before it turns into a clump.

• Sewing machines do require occasional lubrication under normal use. Heavy use of a sewing machine should be followed by proportionately greater lubrication. Check your manual, or ask your dealer for explicit instructions.

Chapter 4

Household Equipment:

How to maintain those things that keep your home running smoothly.

An attic fan, a water heater, and a rack of kitchen utensils may seem to have little in common, but they and a number of other items complete the list of household products discussed in the last three chapters.

The first part of this chapter covers major equipment and the second section details the steps to take to extend the life of your kitchen utensils.

AIR CLEANERS

Electronic air cleaners are often added to a ducted climate control system. Unlike mechanical filters, which catch only large airborne particles, electronic cleaners trap pollutants as small as smoke particles.

• Electronic air cleaners with integral wash facilities should have the cleaner cells washed every two weeks. It is necessary, however, to remove the cells every two or three years and wash them thoroughly in warm, soapy water.

• Those cleaners which do not have an automatic wash feature should be manually cleaned every two weeks. The pre-filter and collecting cells should be thoroughly cleaned. With some models, it is possible to wash the collector cells in a standard home dishwasher. Run the cells through the normal wash cycle. Be sure to replace the cells by matching the air flow directions on the air duct.

ATTIC FAN

Attic fans are installed to draw cool air through the house, and to vent warm air to the outside. If you have yet to install such a fan, it is wise to buy one which will be driven by an AC motor that runs at a relatively high speed. Higher-speed motors are quieter than those that run at slower speeds. High-speed motors are generally connected to the fan by means of a V-belt.

• Anything that makes a motor work harder than it should will shorten its life. If your fan is behind a set of louvers, make sure that they open quickly and the area is big enough to carry away all of the air being pushed by the fan. Also make sure that a door to the attic is open to insure a steady flow of air.

• The fan must be sized to do the job. A fan which is either too small or too large will be inefficient and have to work harder.

• The proper use of an attic fan is also important in getting long life. A fan run during the day, when the outside air is as hot as the air in the house, is a waste of electricity and a step to shortening its life. To get the most from an attic fan, turn it on only in the later afternoon when the outside air begins to cool. Then, only open a few windows on the first floor. Just before bedtime, close the downstairs windows and open the upstairs windows to draw cool air into the bedrooms. Rather than fall asleep and let the fan run all night, it is a good idea to install an automatic timer. Make sure that you get one that is rated to carry the current load to the fan motor. The current rating of the switch of the timer should equal or exceed the current rating of the fan motor. If in doubt, consult your electrical dealer before you buy.

• Some electric motors used to drive fans will require lubrication. Consult the details on the motor nameplate and follow the instructions. It is important that this equipment receive the proper lubrication. Fans are often installed under a hot roof and sit for months at temperatures around 100°.

• If your fan is one which is driven by a separate motor and pulley system, make sure that the pulley bearings are lubricated regularly. But don't get any oil on the surface of the pulley or on the V-belt.

CENTRAL AIR CONDITIONERS

All of the considerations discussed on proper use of room-size air conditioners in Chapter 4 apply to central air conditioning. Efficiency, and long life begin with proper installation and a program of use that doesn't put a strain on the equipment. Refer to this section for details.

• Before performing any of the life-extending maintenance tips discussed below, make sure that the power has been turned off.

• Outdoor condensing units should be cleaned and inspected at the beginning of each cooling season. The condenser coil can be washed down with water from a garden hose.

• Be sure to check the condensate drain on the indoor cooling coil to make sure that the water will run off freely.

• Change the filters on an outdoor unit or blower when they get dirty to prevent the evaporator coil from plugging up. Check filters regularly and when replacement becomes necessary, be sure to get the same size and type of filter.

• Some motors are permanently lubricated and others will require lubrication. As we mentioned earlier, excessive lubrication can be as much of a problem as too little, so rather than try to give you a rule of thumb, we suggest you check the directions that came with the equipment. If you have lost these, the manufacturers will be pleased to send you another set.

• Where there are belt drives with lubricated bearings, lubrication is often required. Make sure that you know whether to use grease or oil and how much is recommended by the manufacturer. If there are no printed instructions, check the dealer who sold you the unit. These fixtures seldom need lubrication more than once a year.

• Check belts at least once a year for wear and slippage. Worn belts should be replaced. The belt should be as loose as possible without allowing any slippage.

HEATING SYSTEMS

To be most effective, and to insure long life, all the parts of a heating system must be kept in top shape. These tips will help you get extra years from your heating plant.

• The oil-burner motor should be lubricated at least two or three times a year (Figure 4-1). Use #10 or #20 oil. The circulating motor and pump in a hot-water system and the blower on a hot-air system should be also oiled regularly. Some newer motors are permanently lubricated, but don't assume this is the case with your system until you've checked.

Figure 4-1: **Some oil-burner motors require regular lubrication. Examine the name plate on the motor and lubricate where and when required. Never overlubricate.**

• A thermostat is strategically located by the builder when the house is constructed. It should be on an inside wall, away from windows and possible drafts and never behind a door. Try to keep the thermostat clear of anything such as a lamp, that will adversely affect its operation. To be safe, it is wise to have a trained serviceman check the thermostat every 4 or 5 years. If it is not operating properly, it can cause the furnace to work harder than it should, and it can waste expensive energy.

• Hot-air heating systems usually have filters installed near the furnace to trap dirt and dust. Check this filter two or three times a year and clean or replace the filter if necessary. A clogged filter will make the blower work harder and it will also begin to dump dirt and dust into the room. This can damage fabrics, paint surfaces, and other things in the room.

• A hot-water system will have to be bled regularly. Air in the water will accumulate at the highest point; such bubbles slow down the flow of hot water. Begin with the highest radiator in the house and gently open the bleed valve. Air will hiss out until water begins to flow. At this point, you will know that you have released all the trapped air. Turn off the valve immediately. Repeat this with all the radiators in the house.

• Believe it or not, the efficiency of a radiator can be cut down quite a bit when it becomes choked with dust. A regular vacuuming of the radiator will make sure that you get your money's worth from the fuel you use.

• Steam radiators have automatic vent valves which allow trapped air to escape to make room for the steam. If these vents fail because of accumulated mineral deposits, the radiator will either be always open, causing loss of steam, or will stay closed, preventing the steam from getting to the radiator. The vent should be removed and boiled in a pan of water for a few minutes. If this does not unclog it, it is best to install a replacement. Test for proper automatic valve action by listening to each valve as the steam comes up. At first you should hear a gentle hiss as the trapped air escapes; then you should hear a snap as the valve closes to trap and contain the warming steam.

HEAT PUMPS

The heat pump is rapidly becoming a practical means toward climate-control in a house. It works on an adaptation of the refrigeration principle, and much of the maintenance is the same as that described for refrigeration equipment.

The outdoor unit. The coil should be cleaned and inspected twice a year. It can be washed down with a garden hose. Most fan motors associated with modern heat pumps are permanently lubricated. On the off-chance that your unit requires lubrication, check the manual, or the name-plate on the motor itself.

Most heat-pump outside units are equipped with an automatic defrost system. This keeps the outdoor coil from icing up, even in cold weather. If ice is noticed, a serviceman should be called to discover the source of the trouble.

Indoor unit. The condensate drain should be checked regularly during the cooling season to make sure the water flows freely. Filters should be checked and cleaned regularly. They can either be vacuumed, or washed in mild detergent water. After drying, the filter should be recoated with an oil spray which is often available from the dealer who sold, or installed, the pump. Lubricable motors should be oiled annually, or as instructed by the manufacturer.

INCINERATORS

Incinerators can be handy appliances, but they should be cared for carefully. High temperatures and flammable gases in a home always bear careful watching. These tips apply to both gas and electric incinerators.

• Never put anything that won't burn in an incinerator. Most service problems are caused by a grate clogged by cans and bottles.

• Shake down the ashes gently, and be sure to open the loading door slightly during the process. If you don't observe these precautions, you might smother the flame.

• Empty the ash drawer before it is completely full. If the drawer is left to fill to the brim, there is a possibility that the air supply to the flame will be cut down. This will result in poor drying action, and extended unnecessary use of the system.

• Drain wet garbage as much as possible, and wrap it in plenty of dry paper before putting it in the chamber.

• Keep the refuse bundles small.

• Allow enough time for a load to be burned before re-loading the chamber. An accumulation cuts the burning efficiency considerably. More gas will be used, and there is a chance of an odor problem occurring.

KITCHEN FANS

Kitchen fans are usually built into the wall to vent outside, or they are incorporated into hoods mounted over stoves. Their main job is to draw the smell, smoke, and airborne grease out of the house.

• Kitchen fans should be cleaned regularly. Any build-up of grease will get progressively more difficult to remove, and it will decrease the efficiency of the fan motor. Be sure you don't accidentally turn the fan on while you are cleaning the blades. Some fans have switches on the frame or grill hub, and it is quite easy to bump the switch on while cleaning.

• Avoid using a very wet cloth to clean the fan. Liquids, or solvents can run into the motor and damage it.

• Liquid, or powdered detergents, washing soda, or ammonia and water will work with the grease build-up on a kitchen fan. A cloth lightly dampened in any of these cleaners will do the job.

WATER HEATER

Water heaters are either gas or electrically operated. These suggestions apply to both.

• If you have hard water in the lines, it is a good idea to install a water softener ahead of the heater. This will prevent the deposition of mineral scale.

• Drain about five gallons of water from the bottom of the tank every month to prevent the build-up of minerals and sludge.

• Keep the tank well insulated. If the tank is not supplied with permanent insulation, wrap-around insulation is available from hardware and plumbing supply stores.

• If your heater uses a gas burner, keep the room ventillated. A gas flame needs air.

• The normal temperature setting is 140°. If you find that you have to set the thermostat higher and higher to maintain the hot water you need, you should have the system serviced by a professional.

WATER SOFTENER

Foods cooked in hard water are often shrivelled and soaps can be rendered virtually useless by extremely hard water. To remove the minerals that make water hard, many people use a commercial water softener. Here are a few tips to help you get the most from your water softener.

• Use only the most pure rock or pellet salt in the water softener.

• Impurities will settle in the bottom of the tank and should be cleaned regularly. The cleaning should be done at least annually, or more, depending on the quantity of salt used and the impurities contained in it.

• If you have a manual, or semi-automatic water softener, be sure to add salt and regenerate the unit as specified by the manufacturer. If this is not done on a rigid schedule, it is possible for hard water to get into the lines and negate much of the work of the softener.

• Impurities can build up in the brine tank that will ultimately insulate the salt from the water. Occasionally, the salt level should be allowed to drop to empty to permit an inspection of the baseplate and removal of the accumulated sludge.

KITCHEN UTENSILS

Kitchen utensils seldom receive any attention except routine cleaning. Because of this, many utensils have to be replaced regularly. These hints will help you get extra years from your kitchen tools.

Cutlery. Cutlery should be thoroughly cleaned immediately after use. Stainless steel knife blades won't stain, but blades made of carbon steel will stain if they are not cleaned thoroughly. Use scouring powder on carbon steel blades for best results.

• Rinse washed cutlery thoroughly to remove soap and detergents.

• Dry knives very carefully before storing them. When water is not wiped away quickly, it can cause the handles to loosen.

- Knives should be stored in such a way that the tips and blades do not touch each other or other kitchen items. This will preserve the cutting edges. A hanging knife rack is best.

- To do their best work, knives should be kept sharp. If you use a wheel or flat stone, hold the blade at about 15° angle with the surface of the stone (Figure 4-2). The common kitchen sharpener which is made up of a series of small wheels forming a "V" can be used. For best results with this device, pull the blade through the "V" a number of times with a steady pressure and stroke. Do not push it back and forth.

Figure 4-2:   **Use a combination coarse- and fine-grit oilstone to sharpen knives. Lubricate the stone with light oil and move the blade back and forth on the coarse side first. Repeat this on the fine side. Burrs can be removed by a few light strokes sideways.**

Pots and Pans. In addition to the prevention of dents and broken handles, pots and pans can be made to last by careful cleaning. These steps will help:

Aluminum pots can be made to keep their shine by avoiding the use of harsh soaps. Use scalding water for the rinse.

• If you happen to burn some food in an aluminum pot, don't try to pick it free with a metal utensil. You'll surely nick it and make crevices that will trap other food. It's best to fill the pot with water and bring it to a boil for a few minutes. Then use either a wooden spoon or plastic pad to work the burned food loose. A very fine steel wool can be used, but this should be done with care. Rub lightly and in only one direction; follow the lines in the surface of spun aluminum pots.

• Do not use harsh abrasives, lye, ammonia and alkalis which can discolor aluminum.

• If you already have a stained aluminum pot, try boiling two teaspoons of cream of tartar in a quart of water for a few minutes.

• Mineral scale forms in pots and kettles used frequently for boiling water. You can get rid of this scale by boiling a half-and-half mixture of vinegar and water for a few minutes. Let the mixture cool in the pot for a few hours and lift the loosened deposit with steel wool.

Copper pots and pans are excellent conductors of heat, but the green formation that often appears on the surface can be poison. For this reason most copper pots today are plated with other metals, such as tin or chromium.

• The green copper oxide should be removed, even if it doesn't appear on a cooking surface. This is best done by rubbing the area with hot vinegar and salt. Rinse thoroughly and let the pot dry.

• If you have a copper pot in which the outer plate has worn, either discard the pot, or have it replated. It could produce a harmful poison.

Stainless steel pots are rust-proof but they can be damaged by rapid heating, or scorched food. Bring stainless pans and pots to the desired temperature slowly, and you'll have no problems.

Glassware. Glassware should last forever, but it's life is most often ended by a fast trip to the floor. These hints will not prevent this kind of damage, but they will help extend the life of your glass utensils.

• Glass cookware can be damaged by thermal shock. That is, don't take a pot from the oven and plunge it into the dishpan. Let it cool to room temperature before washing.

• When you wash utensils, clean the fragile glassware first. Dry it before you put other items in the drying rack.

Chapter 5

The Clothes You Wear:

How to make them look better and last longer.

It's not necessary to become a clothes-nut to get the extra wear; simple things such as hanging clothes immediately after wearing, and seeing that they have room to breathe in your closet will add life and luster. A light brushing of a suit will not only prolong its useful life and appearance, it will also lengthen the time between expensive dry cleaning.

Because clothes are often bought on the basis of style, it is easy to overlook the evaluation of quality, and not to consider the fabric in terms of its anticipated use. This chapter will give you a clear picture of the major fabrics and what you can expect from them. It will also explain the ins-and-outs of labels.

Many of today's fabrics can be cleaned by simple home methods. However, it is easy to damage some fabrics if the cleaning is bungled. This chapter will also show you when and how to clean at home, and tell you when the aid of a professional cleaner should be sought.

FABRICS AND LABELING

In the days when clothing was made only from natural fibers such as wool or cotton, it was a simple matter to select the fabric that best suited the need and to clean it properly. Today, every chemical manufacturer has one or more synthetic materials to offer the clothing manufacturer. These materials require special care, and simply including the name of the material is no longer enough to guide the user in proper selection and care.

In 1967, the Industry Advisory Committee on Textile Information was formed and worked with government agencies to develop a consistent labeling system to insure that the consumer had all the information needed to make an intelligent selection. Here is a summary of the information that is included in the labels of all cooperating clothing manufacturers:

FOR MACHINE WASHABLE FABRICS

Label:	*Meaning:*
Washable Machine washable	Wash, bleach, dry and press by any customary method including commercial laundering
Home launder only	Same as above, but do not use commercial laundering methods
No bleach	Do not use bleach
No starch	Do not use starch
Cold wash, cold setting, cold rinse	Use cold water from tap, or cold washing machine setting
Lukewarm wash, warm wash, warm setting, warm rinse	Use warm water (hand comfortable) 90° to 110° Farenheit
Medium wash, medium setting	Use warm water (medium washing machine setting) 110° to 130° F.
Hot wash, hot setting	Use hot water (hot washing machine setting) 130° Farenheit or hotter.
No spin	Remove wash load before final machine spin cycle
Delicate cycle, gentle cycle	Use appropriate machine setting; otherwise, wash by hand
Durable press cycle, permanent press cycle	Use appropriate machine setting; otherwise use medium wash, cold rinse and short spin cycle
Wash separately	Wash alone, or with like colors

FOR NON-MACHINE WASHING

Label:	*Meaning:*
Hand washable, wash by hand	Launder only by hand in warm water. May be bleached. May be dry-cleaned.
Hand wash only	Same as above, but do not dryclean.
Hand wash separately	Hand wash alone or with like colors
No bleach	Do not use bleach

FOR HOME DRYING

Label:	*Meaning:*
Tumble dry, machine dry	Dry in tumble dryer at specified setting—high, medium, low or no heat.
Tumble dry, remove promptly	Same as above, but in absence of cool-down cycle, remove at once when tumbling stops
Drip dry, hang dry, line dry	Hang wet and allow to dry with hand shaping only
No squeeze, no wring, no twist	Hang dry, drip dry, or dry flat only
Dry flat	Lay garment on flat surface
Block to dry	Maintain original size and shape while drying

FOR IRONING OR PRESSING

Cool iron	Set iron at lowest setting
Warm iron	Set iron at medium setting
Hot iron	Set iron at hot setting
No iron, no press	Do not iron or press with heat

| Steam iron, steam press | Iron or press with steam |
| Iron damp | Dampen garment before ironing |

MISCELLANEOUS

Dry clean, Dryclean only	Garment should be drycleaned only
Professionally clean only, commercially clean only	Do not use self-service dry-cleaning
No dryclean	Use recommended care instructions. No drycleaning materials to be used.

FABRIC INFORMATION

Durable press fabrics. Durable press fabrics have been a boon to the busy housewife and the traveling executive. Garments made of durable press fabrics hold their shape longer, and require little or no pressing. However, it has been found that clothes made from these fabrics will last longer if they are drycleaned, rather than laundered. Drycleaning removes oil and grease completely, reduces color absorption, maintains whiteness, causes less color and strength loss from abrasion, and minimizes shrinkage.

Soil release fabrics. Some fabrics such as those made of polyester fibers and cotton are now treated with soil release agents to make cleaning easier. This treatment works with many staining agents, but there are no chemical treatments that will release stains made by mustard, motor oil, lipstick, grass, butter, tobacco, catsup and coffee. So, don't let the advertising claims lull you into believing that clothes made from fabrics treated with soil release agents can be cleaned every time.

HOW TO BUY CLOTHING

It isn't always necessary to buy the most expensive clothes to get the best wear. These few hints will help you get a start on long life for your clothes.

Colorfastness. Be sure to ask about colorfastness of the fabric you plan to buy. Laundering according to the instructions on the label will help preserve the color of any fabric.

Light sensitivity. Some dyed fabrics will fade in sunlight. To get the most life from fabrics that will be exposed to the sun, make sure that you determine how well the fabrics will stand up to it.

Shrinkage. Most of the synthetics will not shrink when they are laundered, but cotton will definitely shrink when washed. If you buy tight fitting clothing that has not been pre-shrunk, its life may just be one wearing—until it is washed.

Weave density. The more threads to the inch, the denser the fabric, and the more life you can expect from the garment. Also, closely woven fabrics retain their shape better.

Launderability. Understanding the labeling we have just explained will help extend the life of the clothes you buy. However, many garments are granted the Certified Washable Seal from the American Institute of Laundering. A garment bearing this label means that it has passed exacting tests for launderability, shrinkage, colorfastness and numerous other qualities. There are good items of clothing that may not carry this seal, simply because the manufacturer did not submit them to the Institute for testing. To be sure that you get a fabric that will last, it is often desirable to ask for a written guarantee before you buy.

Sizing. Some pieces of clothing look sharp and crisp at the counter. But, at first washing, they may become limp pieces of lifeless cloth; the sizing has been washed out. Sizing is a starch used to give fabric body. Excessive sizing can make a light fabric seem more substantial. To test for this problem before you buy, rub two pieces of the cloth against each other. If a white powdery substance falls out, the fabric has been heavily sized and may loose its life after the first washing.

Reprocessed wool. Even though 100% virgin wool is best, it is still possible to get a fine garment made of reprocessed wool. The label will tell you the percentages of virgin and reprocessed wool. Obviously, the more virgin wool, the better. Test the fabric by squeezing it. It should feel smooth and springy. A rough and lifeless piece of woolen fabric is definitely an inferior grade.

Bonded fabrics, laminates and double cloths. A bonded or laminated fabric should be checked by looking closely at both the face fabric and the lining. Gently pull apart a small part at the seam and look for the adhesive or foam holding the two fabrics together. A two-faced piece of cloth held together with an extra set of yarns is actually a double cloth.

Double cloth cannot separate in washing, but bonded fabrics may part when washed or dry cleaned. A partial separation gives the garment a rippled look; air pockets form giving the garment a lumpy feel. When complete separation takes place only the seams hold the two fabrics together, and no amount of pressing will rebond the cloth. Therefore, ask about the bonding material. If the labels don't give you the information you need, ask for a written guarantee that the bonding will hold during the kind of cleaning you plan for the garment.

Read the tag. Never buy any garment without reading the tag. Save the tag, even though the label sewn in may have most of the information needed for cleaning. The tag often contains additional bits of information that could help prevent use and cleaning disasters.

CARE OF FABRIC

After you have made sure that the clothing you buy meets your wearing needs, you should understand the care of each fabric. Here are some tips on the care of fabrics made from natural and synthetic fibers.

Cotton. Clothing made from cotton can be machine washed and tumble dried, and dry cleaned. You can use either a chlorine or peroxide bleach, but these chemicals can weaken the fibers. A chlorine bleach can cause cotton to yellow. The ironing temperature is about $400°$F.

Linen. Linen can be machine washed, tumble dried and dry cleaned. White linen can be bleached, but bleach will eventually weaken the fibers. A temperature of $400°$F is best.

Silk. Hand laundering is the best way to clean silk, although some silk dyes will "bleed" in washing. Test a portion of the fabric that won't show to determine if washing is possible. Silk can also be dry cleaned. The safest ironing temperature is between $250°$ and $275°$F. Never use a chlorine bleach on silk.

Wool. Launder wool by hand or in a washing machine that has an extremely gentle action. Use only cool water and a mild detergent. Never rub wet wool. Laundered wool garments should be dried flat, or spread over two or three wash lines to distribute the weight. Wool can also be dry cleaned. Press with a cool iron and steam. To remove wrinkles, try hanging the garment over a bathtub filled with hot water. Wool clothing should be brushed gently after each wearing and allowed to rest for 24 hours before being worn again. Wool absorbs odors, so garments should be hung where air can circulate around them. Be sure to moth-proof wool clothing before summer storage.

Acetate. You can hand launder acetate in warm water using gentle agitation. Never soak, wring, or twist garments made of acetate. Dry cleaning can also be used. Acetate fibers melt at high temperatures so be sure to keep your iron between 250 ° and 300°F. Nail polish, paint removers and other household solvents will dissolve acetate.

Triacetate. Machine wash and tumble dry triacetate. Unlike acetate, you can press with a hot iron; 450°F will do nicely.

Acrylic. Acrylic fabrics should be machine washed and tumble dried at low temperatures. It is safe to dry clean clothing made of acrylic fibers. The best ironing temperature is between 300° and 325°F. Either chlorine or peroxide bleaches can be used.

Anidex. Machine wash and tumble dry Anidex at normal settings. Only chlorine bleaches are recommended. The recommended safe ironing temperature is 320°F.

Modacrylic. Modified acrylic fabric should be machine washed in warm water and tumble dried at low temperatures. Remove the Modacrylic garment from the machine just as soon as the tumble cycle stops. A safe ironing temperature lies between 200° and 250°F. Modacrylic can be dry cleaned.

Nylon. Nylon can be machine washed and tumble dried at low temperatures. Bleach only with chlorine bleaches. A safe ironing temperature is between 300° and 375°F.

Polyester. You should machine wash and tumble dry polyester garments. Use only chlorine bleaches. A safe ironing temperature lies between 300° and 350°F. Polyester may also be dry cleaned.

Rayon. Rayon is best cleaned by gentle hand washing in lukewarm water. Squeeze it gently; do not wring or twist. It can also be machine washed and tumble dried. Only chlorine bleach should be used. However, some rayon fabrics will have a resin finish that will discolor when bleached. Check the label if you are unsure.

Rayon will scorch if the iron is too hot; keep the temperature between 300° and 350°F. Rayon can also be dry cleaned.

Spandex. Spandex should be machine washed and tumble dried at low temperatures. Dry cleaning may also be used. Do not use chlorine bleaches. Never let the iron temperature go above 300°F, and do not keep the iron on one spot too long.

Blended and combined fibers. Many modern fabrics are a product of blending or combination. A blended fabric is made of fibers that have been blended together before being spun into yarn. In a combination, individual yarns composed of one fiber are combined during weaving with yarns composed of another fiber. Care of blends and combinations can be a problem. Save the hang tags and instructions and clean as directed. However, if you've lost the instructions, the safest thing to do is to clean according to the most sensitive fiber in the blend or combination. Refer to the cleaning instructions given in the previous pages for various fabrics to help solve this problem.

HOW TO CARE FOR YOUR CLOTHES

These simple hints will help you get the most wear out of your clothes . . . . . At least until the style changes.

• Give your clothes the once-over after each wearing. Soils and stains can be removed much more easily when fresh.

• Hang up your clothes as soon as you are finished wearing them. This will help them keep their shape. Try to avoid the wire hangers from the dry cleaner. These hangers are only for transportation purposes; shaped wooden hangers will give your clothes the shape and support they need.

• If possible, let your clothes hang near an open window or other source of fresh air before putting them in a closet. Most odors can be eliminated by this simple step.

• When you do hang your clothes in a closet, give them breathing room. Clothes packed tightly will pick up odors from other clothes in the same closet, and all the clothing will be crushed and wrinkled. (Figure 5-1.)

• Make sure pocket flaps are down before hanging clothes in a closet to prevent wrinkling.

Figure 5-1:   **This messy closet wrinkles clothes, traps odors, and transfers dust and grime from one garment to another.**

• Make sure there is nothing in your clothes closet that can impart an odor to your clothes. Golf clubs, fishing tackle and other sports equipment all have odors that can be picked up by clothing very quickly.

• Your clothes closet should be dry and cool and have some air circulation. A warm, moist closet will encourage mildew, especially if your clothing contains any starch. Mildew is difficult to remove, and must be bleached. Unless the fabric can withstand bleaching, you might not be able to remove the mildew.

• Give your clothes a regular brushing to get rid of dust, lint, hair and other damaging particles. Be sure to brush in the direction of the nap. Empty the pockets of lint and turn the cuffs inside-out at the same time. (Figure 5-2.)

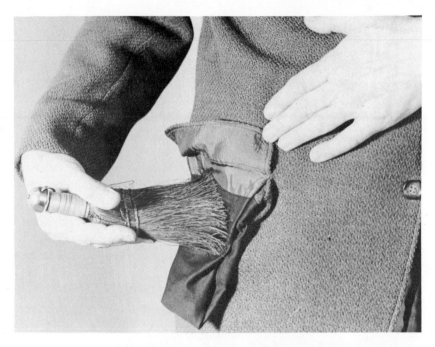

Figure 5-2:   **Brush out jacket and trouser pockets regularly and before sending the garments to the cleaners.**

• Cleaning stubborn spots from clothing is best left to a professional dry cleaner, but here's a tip on the most often soiled piece of men's clothing—the tie. Food stains can often be lifted if a little talcum powder is lightly rubbed into the stain and the tie left to dry overnight. A gentle brushing in the morning will often remove the spot.

• A garment should never be left to hang uncleaned from one season to the next. Stains will set to the point where it will be impossible to remove them. Other soils will attract moths.

• Avoid applying perfumes, colognes and deodorants directly to clothing. Some fabrics will dissolve on contact with these chemicals. Other deodorant chemicals will weaken fibers when combined with heat applied by ironing. Play it safe—keep deodorants away from outer garments.

• Sweaters and other knitted garments should be stored flat in a drawer, and not on hangers.

CLEANING TIPS

Anything that can be washed at home is relatively easy to care for. A review of the past few pages on fabrics and labeling information will help you decide how to clean your clothes. However, it's the catsup and anchovy type of stains that cause problems. It is tempting to try to remove them yourself, but you can often do more harm than good. You may get the spot out, but you may also get some of the fabric color along with the spot. Leave the spot removal to the professionals. But, if you do get a spot, here are some first-aid tips to help solve some of the problems.

• Never use heat on any stain. No matter what you spill on cloth, a hot iron will set it.

• Never rub the spot. It's tempting to try to rub the spot with either water or a cleaning agent. This rubbing only chafes the fabric and may damage the color of the cloth.

• Have a professional remove the stain as quickly as possible. Just the warmth of a closet or a bureau drawer can set a stain. Be sure to tell the cleaner just what caused the stain, and what the fabric is. With this knowledge, the cleaner can make sure that you get a lot more wear from the clothing—without the stain.

STAIN REMOVAL FIRST AID

When you can't get to a dry cleaner, you can try some of these techniques. Even if you can't remove the entire stain, you may be able to get enough off so that later dry cleaning will be able to finish the job completely.

Alcoholic beverages. Lightly sponge the stain with water. Then pour liquid detergent over the stain and let it rest for half an hour. Rinse completely.

Berry stains. Rinse thoroughly in hot water. This seldom gets all the stain out, but it's the best first aid until you can get to a dry cleaner.

Blood. A cold water soaking followed by a sponging with lukewarm, sudsy water will often do the trick. Never use hot water.

Butter. Warm sudsy water will get most of a butter stain out. Non-washable fabrics should be sponged lightly with dry-cleaning fluid.

Candy. Washable fabrics should be cleaned in warm, sudsy water. Use lukewarm clear water for non-washable fabrics.

Chewing gum. Scrape the excess gum with a dull knife. Be careful not to scrape and weaken the fabric fibers. Try rubbing the remaining gum with an ice cube until the gum rolls up into a ball that can be picked off. Sponge the remaining stain with dry-cleaning fluid.

Chocolate. Soak the fabric in cold borax water for about an hour, and then rinse thoroughly.

Coffee. First rinse the spot in cold water. Follow this with a hot water rinse. If the stain remains, you can try a mixture of one part peroxide (from the drug store) and three parts water.

Cosmetics. Waxy cosmetics will occasionally respond to a light rubbing with a piece of bread. Most cosmetic stains can only be removed by a professional.

Crayon. First apply drycleaning fluid, then wash in hot water. The wax will be removed, but the dyes may remain. This is a problem for the dry cleaner.

Egg. After removing excess egg with a dull knife, wash the fabric in warm, sudsy water.

Glue. Try a ten minute soak in warm, sudsy water. Rinse in warm water. There are so many different glues that it is impossible to give complete instructions on removal. Your best bet is professional dry-cleaning.

Grass stains. A washable fabric can often be cleaned of grass stains by using undiluted liquid detergent, and rubbing the fabric between the hands. Do not rub the fabric against itself. For fabrics that require dry-cleaning, either see a professional, or use dry-cleaning fluid.

Grease. Lightly rub corn starch into the spotted area. Brush off and repeat the process until you get all that will come off with this treatment. The balance of the stain can often be removed with a light sponging of cleaning fluid.

Ink, ball point. Cover the stain with liquid detergent and then rinse. Dry the fabric and blot the remaining spot with dry-cleaning fluid.

Ink, writing. Wash with cold water, using no soap. Follow this by a second washing of warm, sudsy water. If the stain remains, a treatment of diluted bleach will help. Two teaspoons of bleach to a cup of water is about right for this stain.

Iodine. A teaspoon of sodium thiosulphate in a cup of warm water will remove an iodine stain. The treatment should be followed by a thorough rinse. You can get sodium thiosulphate at a drug store or photo shop.

Meat. A cold water soak before a thorough laundering is best for this stain. Never use hot water for the soak; it will set the stain.

Rust. Use any commercial rust remover—but never use liquid bleach. Rust activates the bleach to the point where it might eat a hole in the cloth.

Scorching. Try a light bleaching, if the fabric will tolerate it. You might also try dampening the scorched area and placing it in bright sunlight, or under a home sun lamp for about ten minutes.

Shoe polish. Alcohol will dissolve the wax in a shoe polish. Never use alcohol on acetates.

Soot. Dampen the spot with liquid detergent and rub the fabric between your hands. Rinse and repeat until the stain has been removed.

Spot-remover stains. Ever try to remove a stain with dry-cleaning fluid only to find that the fluid spread out and left a ring on the fabric? It's a common problem and can often be remedied by holding the stained area over the steam from a boiling kettle. Make sure that the fabric will take this kind of treatment. Read the label and refer to the previous pages of this chapter for details on the various fabrics.

Tar. Try to scrape off most of the tar with a dull knife. Be sure that you don't damage the cloth surface. When the bulk of the tar has been lifted, sponge the area with dry-cleaning fluid and blot immediately with a paper towel. Repeat these steps until no more of the tar stain appears on the paper towel. There still may be a stain on the fabric which will require professional attention.

Tea. If the fabric is colorfast and washable, rinse the spot in very hot water. Any remaining stain can be further treated with a dilute of bleach. Be sure the fabric can be bleached.

CARING FOR FURS

Fur coats require special care. But the care taken will protect the investment made in a fur.

• Keep furs away from heat—radiators, steam pipes and long exposures to sunlight. Heat dries the fur and causes the leather to become brittle.

• Fur coats should never be brushed or combed. Shake them out after each wearing.

• Avoid carrying a handbag over a fur sleeve habitually. This can wear the area and permanently damage the fur.

• Damp furs should be hung in a cool, dry place. There should be some circulating air, so a closet is not the best place. A fur that has been thoroughly soaked in the rain should be taken to a furrier for proper treatment.

• Broad-shouldered hangers are best for hanging furs.

• Give the fur coat lots of space in the closet.

• Furs should be cleaned regularly by a furrier. Fur cleaning is not a task for the amateur.

• Off-season storage is best handled by a furrier. Never store a fur in an air-tight plastic bag. The fur needs a circulation of air to prevent it from drying out. Furs stored in modern storage vaults are kept at the right temperature and humidity and they are professionally protected from moths.

• Never pin jewelry directly to a fur.

CARING FOR LEATHER GLOVES

Leather gloves are more costly than other gloves, but they will last longer than gloves made of other materials. Follow these hints and you can get extra years from your leather gloves.

• Just putting a glove on properly will extend its life considerably. First, turn the glove wrist down and slip in your fingers. Then, push your thumb in place and gently draw the rest of the glove over your wrist. (Figure 5-3.)

• Remove the glove by turning down the wrist and gently drawing it backwards, wrong-side out. Never put excess strain on any part of the glove.

• Once removed, gloves should be drawn back to their normal shape and stored flat, palms together in a drawer free from dust. Damp gloves should be allowed to air dry before being stored.

• The natural oils in human skin help to keep leather gloves in top condition.

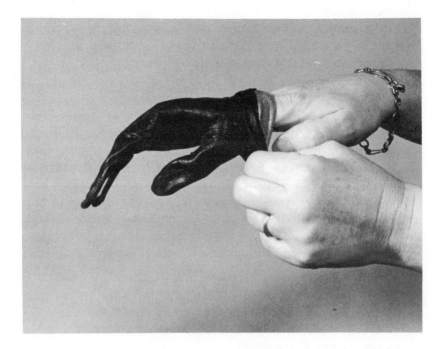

Figure 5-3:   **Putting on a glove properly will make it last and last.**

• Most leather gloves can be washed, but a glove that has been dry cleaned should never be washed. Wash in luke-warm to cool, mild, soap suds. Change the water until the gloves are clean. Rinse thoroughly. Chamois and doeskin gloves should be washed while on the hand and rinsed in clean soap suds. Other types of leather gloves are washed off the hand and rinsed in clear luke-warm water. Never wring out a washed leather glove or dry it near a radiator. Blot wet gloves with towels to soak up most of the water. Then shape them and let them lie flat at room temperature until fully dry. When the gloves are fully dry, you can soften them by rubbing between moistened fingertips.

• Sport gloves, such as those worn to play golf, should be allowed to dry in the open before they are stored. The excess perspiration and acid from the hands can ruin them quickly. You can greatly extend the life of golf gloves with an occasional rub of saddle soap.

• Ski gloves seldom return from a day on the slopes in anything but a soaked condition. Never try to dry them in a hurry on a hot radiator; air dry them at room temperature.

CARING FOR LEATHER CLOTHING

There are two kinds of leather clothing popular today—suede and grain or smooth leather. Actually, the difference is in the tannery process that finishes them, and not in the animal from which the pelts are taken. Suede leather is a hide that is buffed to raise a velvety nap. This buffing is usually done on the underside of the hide, but it is occasionally done to the top, or grain side. Grain leather is treated with dyes and finishes on the top side to make it look and feel smooth.

There are a few precautions that you should observe with both kinds of leather:

• Wear a scarf whenever possible to protect a leather neckline from hair preparations and the natural oils of human hair.

• Hang the leather garment between wearings in a place where the air circulates freely.

• A damp or wet garment should be dried slowly at room temperature. Don't try to speed up the process by placing the garment over a hot radiator.

• Don't let leather clothes become too soiled before they are cleaned. Except for routine care (described below) stain removal should be left to the professional.

• Stains and dyes used to color leather and suede are often removed by the dry-cleaning process. Therefore, such garments must be redyed after each cleaning. This cost should be considered when purchasing a leather garment.

• All pieces of a matching leather ensemble should be cleaned together. This will insure that they will continue to match.

Suede Leather, also known as split leather should be treated carefully. These hints will help extend the life of your suede garments.

• Brush suede clothes regularly with a clean terry-cloth towel or a special suede brush. This will prevent dust from settling in the nap. (Figure 5-4.)

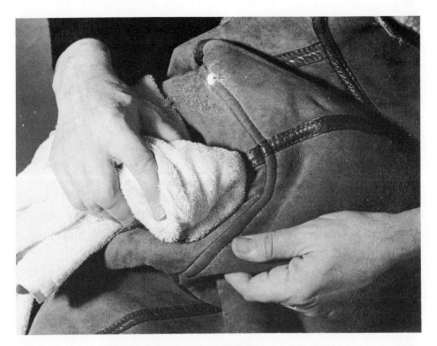

Figure 5-4: Brush suede regularly with a terry-cloth towel to remove dirt and to loosen the knap.

• Spots and light stains can often be removed by using a soft gum eraser or a piece of fine emery paper. Deep stain and resistant spots should be attended to by a professional. Do not use home dry-cleaners and sprays.

• Wet and rain-spotted suede leather should be allowed to dry away from heat in a well-ventilated area. When it is fully dry, a light buffing with a dry terry-cloth towel will restore the original appearance.

• You can press a suede garment, but you must use caution. Set the iron at its lowest temperature; never use steam. Use a press cloth, or a piece of heavy brown paper, between the iron and the surface of the suede. Keep the iron moving; never leave it on one spot. After the garment has been pressed, you should brush it gently with a terry-cloth towel, or a suede brush.

• Remove accidental spillage of food before it has a chance to dry. Use a soft cloth dampened in cool water to remove any of the residual stain. Never rub with the cloth—blot! Dry the dampened area with paper or terry-cloth towels and let air dry. When the spot has thoroughly dried, brush the surface to revive the velvet look.

Smooth and grained leather responds to home care and will give years of service with only a little attention.

- A damp cloth and a mild soap will clean most spots from grain leather. Don't use home cleaning fluids, shoe creams, or saddle soap.
- Wet grain leather garments should be allowed to dry in a warm, ventilated spot. Avoid excessive heat, such as a radiator.
- Wrinkled grain leather can be smoothed by an overnight hanging in a damp room. A closed bathroom, after a hot shower has been an ideal spot. A light pressing with an iron at the rayon setting will get out the most persistent wrinkles. Use heavy brown wrapping paper between the iron and the leather and press on the finished side of the garment. Light, quick strokes are important; never let the iron sit on the spot.
- Cover a leather garment with a cloth for off-season storage to keep dust away. Do not store in a plastic bag.

CARING FOR HOSIERY

Pantyhose has all but replaced separate stockings. There are many benefits, but they must be used and washed carefully to assure long life.

- Select the right size. A size smaller or larger will hasten their demise. Follow the weight-height chart available from most hosiery manufacturers for retail use.
- Put pantyhose on by first gathering the fabric of each leg and slipping in both feet. Then, fit the stocking part up over each knee. Next, stand up and work the fabric over each leg. Make sure that the fabric is evenly distributed, but don't pull or yank. Then work the panty portion over your hips for a comfortable fit. If you don't get a comfortable fit the first time, don't try to readjust the fabric. Simply remove the pantyhose and start from the ankles again.

• Guard against rough hands and nails; this is the fastest way to get a run in the fabric.

• Pantyhose should be gently hand-washed in mild soap suds at a moderate temperature. Place them on a towel over a shower rod or the edge of a tub and allow them to dry thoroughly. Pantyhose should be washed carefully after each wearing.

• Don't stand directly behind an automobile exhaust. The fumes can cause nylon to weaken or deteriorate.

CARING FOR SHOES

Leather shoes should be treated with the same care we described for leather clothing. However, these few additional hints will extend the life and enhance the beauty of your shoes.

• Keep your shoes polished with a good wax finish. For best results, first clean them with a dry cloth and a bristle brush. An occasional application of saddlesoap will greatly extend the life of your shoes.

• If your shoes require a little wiggling to get into, always use a shoehorn.

• Suede shoes should be brushed regularly with a stiff brush. Avoid a metal brush that might cause serious scratches. There are coarse brushes made of fine metal bristles that are fine for this application. (Figure 5-5.)

• Scuff marks on suede shoes can be removed, or at least made less noticeable, by rubbing with a cloth or brush dampened in vinegar. When the dampened area has dried, buff it up with a suede brush.

• Damp shoes should be dried inside to avoid problems of mildew. Drying is best handled by using the cold air setting of a hair dryer or the exhaust part of a vacuum cleaner.

• Water-soaked shoes should be stuffed with newspapers and left to dry at room temperature. Don't try to hasten the drying with heat.

• Shoes have a tendency to change shape when not being worn. If they are left for more than a few days, the shape may become permanent and very uncomfortable. This can be prevented by placing shoe trees in them when they are not being worn.

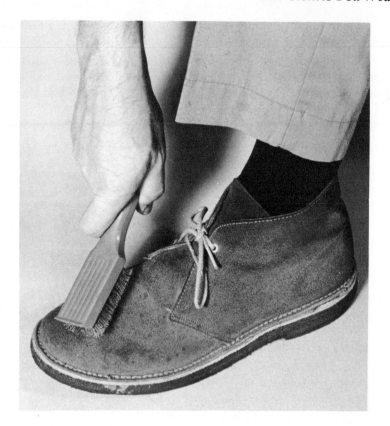

Figure 5-5:   **Brush suede shoes regularly to keep them fresh. Spots can be removed with fine sandpaper or steel wool.**

• If you plan to have your shoe life extended by replacing heels and soles, don't let the heel or sole wear to the point where other parts of the shoe must be replaced. It may then cost more than the shoe is worth.

Chapter 6

Your Automobile:

How to get more miles for less money.

Your automobile is made up of a number of separate systems which must function together. If any system is out of adjustment, it can affect the others and reduce the useful life of the car. For example, a simple thing such as under-inflated tires can waste as much as one mile per gallon of gasoline, affect the steering mechanism, and produce heat in the rubber that can shorten tire life. It's a simple matter to check tire pressure and other automobile systems regularly to make sure they are performing as they should. Not only will you get more miles from your car, you will also drive in greater comfort.

Many of the checks we describe can be performed by anyone. Most of the adjustments can be made with a few inexpensive tools; other adjustments require the care of a professional. But when you know what to look for, you can seek the help of an experienced mechanic for the more difficult jobs.

In addition to checking your automobile and making adjustments, it is important to know how to drive an automobile to get the most for your money. Surprisingly, there is a lot more to driving than the simple steps outlined in most drivers' manuals.

DRIVING

Today, good driving skills are very important; they can help you get the most of the very expensive gasoline you use. It has been estimated that the difference between good and poor driving habits can amount to savings of as much as $500 to $600 a year.

Starting. When you start your car, you are putting a heavy strain on the battery and starter motor, especially in cold weather. These tips will help you get the most from these systems and extend the life of your car.

• Automatic transmission cars can only be started when the shift lever is in park or neutral. However, many manual-shift cars can be started with the gear shift lever in any position. If you start with the manual shift in any gear position, be sure the clutch is depressed. It is best to start with the shift lever in neutral, and with the clutch depressed.

• If you have difficulty starting the engine, rather than wear down the battery, have a service attendant check for the trouble.

• In warm weather it is not necessary to let the engine warm up completely before driving. However, in cold weather, the oil will thicken and it is best to wait until the engine heat has lightened the oil.

• Do not let your car run at a fast idle for more than 5 minutes. If your car is equipped with an automatic choke, quickly depressing and releasing the accelerator will release the choke, and reduce the idle speed. Push in the manual choke if your car is equipped with this system.

• If you notice that your starter turns the motor over more slowly than before, check your battery. It could be low on water and require filling, or it could be at the end of its life. See the section on batteries for maintenance tips.

Driving. These driving tips will help you extend car life as well as save you money on your gasoline bill.

• Avoid "jackrabbit" starts. Rapid acceleration, whether from a standstill or from a lower speed puts a heavy strain on the engine, and the rest of the power train which delivers the energy to the drive wheels. It also gulps gasoline at a frightful rate.

• Cars with automatic transmissions handle the shifting for you, but with a stick shift, you should be careful to shift from a lower gear to a higher gear only when the car will run smoothly in the higher gear. You can only find this point by trying various speeds with your particular car. Shifting to a higher gear before you reach the right point will result in bucking, which can damage the engine and other power-train parts, and it can result in poor fuel economy. You are better off shifting at speeds slightly higher than optimum when accelerating. A smooth, coordinated motion of the gas pedal and the clutch will insure the proper transition from one gear to the next. You will feel this when there is no jerking as you shift gears. This smooth motion will definitely prolong the life of your clutch, and save engine wear.

• Once you are moving, keep your foot on the floor, except when changing gears. Resting your foot on the clutch will cause it to wear rapidly.

• When slowing down in a car with a manual shift, let the engine help the brake. When you take your foot off the gas pedal, the engine will want to run more slowly than it ran to keep you moving. This will put a drag on the drive wheels and help you slow down. As the car reaches lower speeds, down-shift to the next lower gear until it becomes necessary to disengage the motor completely, and put the shift lever in neutral. Do this as smoothly as you shift when accelerating and you will easily double the life of your brakes.

• Some drivers have a habit of stepping on the clutch just as soon as they decide to stop and to use the brake only to stop the car. This puts a very heavy strain on the brakes and will wear them prematurely. It also will leave you without control of the car if you should need power immediately. A car handles better when there is a slight amount of power applied to the drive wheels.

• Avoid sudden stops. If you can anticipate your stops, begin to slow the car by taking your foot off the gas pedal and down-shifting as you approach the stop. Sudden stops generate heat in the brakes which hastens wear. And, it is necessary to use more gasoline to get back to driving speed if you do not come to a complete stop.

• Try to maintain a steady speed. If you can anticipate stoplights ahead so that you merely slow a bit, rather than come to a complete stop, you will help increase the life of your car, and you will have to work less at driving.

• Avoid high speeds. High speeds will wear your car much more rapidly than lower speeds, and higher speeds require considerably more gas. For example, you will use approximately 50% more gasoline if you drive at 70 miles per hour than at 50 miles per hour. The slower you drive, the less gas you will use per mile, but, don't carry this too far and become a slow-moving hazard for other drivers. Obey the speed rates and you will be safe, save fuel, and extend the life of your car.

• If your car has an automatic transmission, it should be placed in "park" when the car is not being used. You should also set the parking brake. Don't depend on either alone.

• When parking on a hill, turn your wheels toward the curb. This will give you added safety, and reduce the strain on the brakes.

• Don't use your automobile trunk as a storage area. Added weight requires more gasoline to move the car, and will also shorten the life of the springs and shock absorber under the trunk. A full tank of gasoline will also add enough weight to be felt in the same way. If you are not taking a long trip where fuel stations may be few and far between, it is best to fill the tank between one-half and three-quarters and refill when you reach one-quarter of a tank. This means more stops at the gasoline station, but it will also contribute to extending the life of your car.

• Be alert to the instruments and signals on your dashboard. Most modern automobiles have replaced the gauges which registered battery charging, oil pressure and water temperature with on-off warning lights. If any of these lights go on, it is an immediate danger signal.

• If the water temperature goes into the danger area, or if the indicator bulb goes on, the car should be stopped immediately and the engine turned off. Open the hood carefully to allow cooler air to circulate around the engine. Don't be too quick to check the radiator by lifting the filler cap. Most cars today have pressurized systems and the added pressure created by an overheated engine could result in a bad scald when the cap is removed. Call a service station to be on the safe side. If you must drive, wait until the engine cools and then drive only short distances with rest pauses for the engine to cool.

• If the oil pressure or generator light comes on, stop the car, turn off the motor and seek professional help immediately. This is a warning of the possibility of serious problems.

MAINTENANCE

There is no reason why you can't get at least 100,000 miles from your automobile without serious or major repairs. Simple maintenance on your part and occasional professional tune-ups will help you achieve this goal.

• *Changing oil and oil filters.* A properly lubricated engine means less friction on the moving parts. Dirty oil can add to the wear and reduce the life of your engine. You should change oil every 3,000 miles, or more frequently if it gets dirty and gritty sooner. You can check oil condition by wiping some oil off the measuring dipstick, or by tapping a sample from the filler plug underneath the engine at the bottom of the oil pan. Most auto manufacturers recommend that oil filters be changed every other oil change, or 6,000 miles.

Changing oil is simply a matter of draining the old oil and replacing it with new. But there are some precautions to observe. The drain plug is located under the engine in what is called the oil pan. Be sure to have a container large enough under this plug to catch all of the dirty oil. A warm engine will drain faster than a cold one, and it's a good idea to wait about 10 minutes to make sure all of the old oil is out. Never start the engine without oil.

Replace the plug and fill the engine with the recommended amount of fresh oil. The oil filler pipe is located in the engine compartment. If you have replaced the filter, the engine will probably need an extra quart; that's about how much the filter normally holds.

If you replace the filter, it should be screwed on hand tight; never use a wrench on this part. It may be necessary, however, to use a wrench to remove the old filter. Special wrenches are available for this purpose and seldom cost more than a few dollars. A little oil should be wiped on the surface of the seal of the oil filter before it is fitted to the car.

Try to use oil produced by the same company. Mixing oils can combine additives made by different manufacturers that may produce harmful results. Look for "SD" on the can; this rating assures you that the oil has passed the tests required for new car use. "SE" on the can indicates that the oil is best used for cars that will pull trailers or make long trips at high speed.

Unless you plan to change oil weights (viscosity) as the seasons change, it is best to use a top quality multigrade oil. The 10-30 weight is most common and can be used safely in temperate climates. Oils used in areas of extreme cold must be light, and your gas station owner can best advise you. Never let the oil level go below "add one quart". Have the gas station attendant check your oil every time you get gas. It is good insurance.

Air filter. The air filter keeps grit out of your engine. This grit can seriously damage cylinder walls and reduce the life of your car. The air filter is located on top or ahead of the carburetor. It can usually be removed by lifting the cover of the filter housing. This cover is most often secured by a simple wing nut. (Figure 6-1).

Paper air filters can be blown clean, using the air hose at your neighborhood service station. Those filters made of polyfoam can be washed in a solvent such as benzene, followed by a bath of soap and water. The polyfoam element should be covered with a light film of oil before it is replaced. The "steel wool" type of filter used in older cars should be treated in the same manner as the polyfoam filter.

Figure 6-1: **This paper oil filter can be cleaned by blowing air through the elements. Plastic filters should be cleaned with a solvent followed by soap and water.**

Even though paper air filters can be blown clean, new elements should be installed every 12,000 miles. When an air filter becomes clogged it can contribute to the problem of gas gobbling, and upset the normal function of the engine.

The battery. Battery care is easy. Just watch the water level, and top up each cell to the indicated level as required. It's best to use distilled water. This is available in gallon jugs in most supermarkets for use in steam irons. Don't overfill the cells.

Every 4,000 or 5,000 miles ask a service station attendant to check the battery's condition while you are getting gas. He will use a hydrometer to do this. This instrument looks like a cook's gravy separator with a hose attached to the end. This check will give you a picture of the specific gravity of the battery electrolyte. In simple terms, the attendant can tell you how healthy your battery is.

The battery electrolyte is an acid, and the fumes will often cause a whitish deposit around the electrical connectors on the battery. If left uncleaned, this deposit can prevent your car from getting all the energy it needs from the battery. The wires should be loosened from the terminals and removed for complete cleaning. First brush away the loose white powder, and then scrub the battery terminal post and the connector with a solution of either ammonia or baking soda in water. There will be a lot of frothing; this is to be expected as the acid sulfate is neutralized by the baking-soda solution. Make sure caps are on tight. Don't get soda inside the battery.

After you have dried the terminals and connectors, replace and tighten them securely to the posts. A light coat of grease, or petroleum jelly, over the entire connection will make it difficult for this sulfate to form in the future. (Figure 6-2.)

Never smoke or use an open flame near an automobile storage battery. Vapors are produced by the electrolytic action that can explode when ignited.

Cooling system. An internal combustion engine develops its power by exploding a mixture of air and gasoline within the cylinders. This causes heat, and excessive heat will damage an engine. Some engines are air-cooled, but most are water cooled. It is important to keep this system functioning properly, and this can be done quite easily.

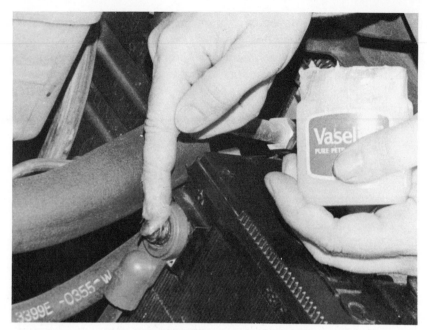

Figure 6-2:   **A light application of grease or petroleum jelly on cleaned battery terminals will prevent corrosion.**

The ethyl-glycol type of antifreeze was formulated to be used in an engine year-round. The best way to use this antifreeze is by mixing 40% water with 60% antifreeze. It's less expensive than using pure antifreeze and it actually protects to a lower temperature. If you want to do the best possible job for your cooling system, use distilled water, rather than ordinary tap water.

It isn't necessary to drain and replace this kind of antifreeze annually. Simply maintain a 60/40 mixture and top off the cooling system as it is required. Make and store a mixture of 6 pints of antifreeze and 4 pints of water. Inspect the radiator level every two or three weeks. To keep the system, including the water pump, in good shape, add a can of rust inhibitor and pump lubricant each year.

The whole cooling system should be flushed about every three years. You can do this yourself, or have your garage do it for you. If you decide to tackle the task yourself, get one of the kits of chemicals developed specially for the job. Complete instructions will accompany each kit.

The hoses that connect the radiator to the engine are subject to chemical and physical wear. You can spot the wear that accompanies flexing, but it is impossible to see what is happening inside the hose. When you have the cooling system flushed every three years, have the hoses and clamps inspected and replaced if need be. (Figure 6-3.)

A thermostat in the system regulates the temperature of the water. It, too, should be inspected every three years when the cooling system is flushed. Overheating or underheating is a definite indication of problems with this component.

Drive belts. A number of belts are used to power such things as generators, alternators, water pumps, air conditioners, and power pumps for steering and braking. The neglect of these belts can cause considerable wear and inefficient operation of other power components.

All belts should be inspected every three or four months. Look for wear and frayed areas. Belts that show any wear will wear further quickly and should be watched closely or replaced immediately.

Figure 6-3: **Check cooling-system hoses regularly. When you see cracks developing, replace the hose immediately.**

Figure 6-4:   **Check drive-belt tension by grasping the belt in the middle and pushing and pulling. If the belt can be moved more than a half inch either way, it should be tightened. Look for worn spots and replace a worn belt.**

The main cause for belt wear is improper adjustment. If you can move the belt midway between two pulleys more than one-half inch (Figure 6-4), the belt should be tightened. This is usually done by loosening a bolt which holds either the part being driven or an idler pulley so that the pulley can be tightened to take up the slack.

Nicked pulleys and pulleys packed with grit will also hasten belt wear. Keep your pulleys clean.

PCV Valve. The Positive Crankcase Ventilation valve reroutes crankcase fumes back to the engine to be burned. When this valve fails, your engine will lose power, idle roughly, and contaminate your oil.

One part of the PCV system is found in a hose routed from the air filter to the oil-filter tube. Pull one end of this hose off while the engine is idling and check for a vacuum. There should be a suction at both ends of this hose. If not, look for obstructions in the hose and the connections.

Another hose in this system can be found running between the rocker-valve cover and the base of the carburetor. The PCV valve is usually located in this length of hose. Check this hose for a vacuum and also examine the valve itself for a possible obstruction. A quick check of the PCV valve will reveal a rattle when it is shaken if it is OK. If it's gummed up, there will be no rattle.

Automatic choke. The automatic choke provides a rich mixture (more gasoline) per volume of air for cold-weather starts. It's thermostatically controlled, but a quick pressing and release of the gas pedal will disengage it.

This device should seldom give you any grief, but if it does, it can cause poor gas mileage and add carbon to your engine. It should be checked when you bring your car in for its regular tune-up. Should it stick, it's a simple matter to take care of the problem. Remove the air cleaner above the carburetor to expose the butterfly valve (a metal disc on a pivot in the pipe below the air cleaner). Spray the pivot points and the disc itself with a solvent such as alcohol, benzine, or special choke cleaner, and work it open and closed a few times until it loosens. Do not oil the pivot points—ever.

Brakes. Don't try to make any adjustments of the brakes unless you possess the right skills. Brake failure can have serious results.

However, it is easy to keep tabs on your brake condition so that professional service can be performed before any serious trouble takes place.

If you notice that your brake pedal is working closer and closer to the floor, it could mean a lack of adjustment or a loss of brake fluid. To check for leakage, park the car, and press hard on the brake pedal for several minutes. Then check the ground around all the wheels for a sign of leaking brake fluid. Also look at the master cylinder which is usually positioned on the fire wall, under the hood, and inspect all the hoses connecting the system. If leaks are found, don't try to drive the car to a service station. A small leak can turn into a big one in seconds and leave you with no brakes at all. Call a tow truck.

If you discover no leaks, it just might mean that the brakes only need adjustment. Many new cars have self-adjusting brakes. To adjust these brakes, drive the car slowly in reverse and press down often and vigorously on the brake pedal. When the brake pedal comes back to its original position, the job has been done.

You can check the level of brake fluid by removing the cover of the reservoir (Figure 6-5). The reservoir can be a separate unit, or it can be part of the master cylinder. In either case, the level should not be below about 1/2 inch from the top. Add brake fluid to this level, and replace the cover securely.

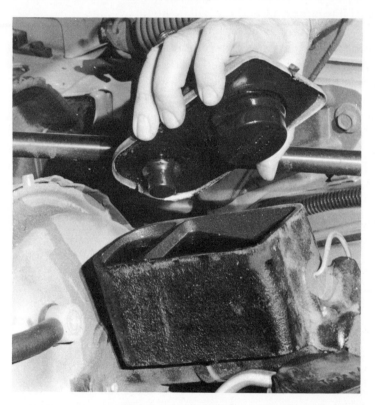

Figure 6-5:   **Check to see if brake-fluid level is one half inch from the top. Be sure the cylinder cover is replaced tightly.**

Spark plugs. Checking and regapping spark plugs should be done at every tune-up (each 6,000 miles) by a professional mechanic. You may want to check them yourself between tune-ups, but the procedure will require a few special tools.

Don't try to remove a spark plug with an ordinary wrench. The porcelain can be damaged very easily. A special wrench that fits over the entire plug and is protected inside is needed. You will also need a feeler gauge to measure and bend the electrodes.

Every automobile will have its own specifications for the gap of its spark plugs. Check your owner's manual, or ask the dealer for the information. When you have removed the plug, first clean the electrode and internal insulation carefully with a wire brush or some steel wool. Be careful not to leave any pieces of steel wool packed inside the plug.

After determining what the gap should be, select the appropriate wire, or blade from the gauge and place it between the electrodes (Figure 6-6). If it fits comfortably, leave the plug alone. If the distance is incorrect, use the little hooked end to gently bend the electrode to make the right gap distance.

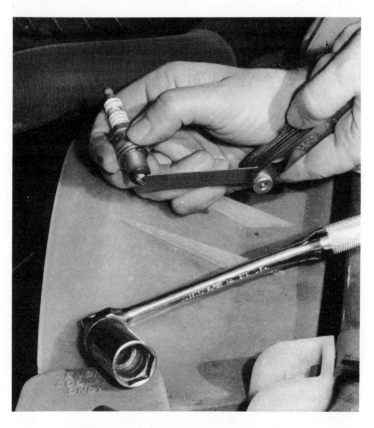

Figure 6-6:   **Using a spark-plug feeler gauge, check the gap on every plug. Where required, adjust to the correct gap. Check your owners' manual for the correct setting.**

Wipe the outside of the plug, and replace it carefully. You should hand-tighten the plug to insure that there are no crossed threads before you apply a wrench for the final tightening.

To make sure that you don't mix up the ignition wires, work on one plug at a time.

Lubrication. The automobile is a mass of parts which rub against each other. We have already discussed the importance of proper engine lubrication, and now it is important to discuss the lubrication of other parts.

Such simple things as door hinges should receive a squirt of light oil every year, and the hinges that connect the hood and trunk hatch should also be oiled.

The generator, or alternator, and other moving parts of your car will also require periodic lubrication. Because it is impossible to give general instructions that will apply to all automobiles, it is best to refer to your owner's manual.

Automatic transmission fluid. If the liquid of the automatic transmission falls below its safe level, serious damage may occur to the transmission. Check the level each time you change oil to be safe.

The engine should be well warmed-up, running, and parked on a level surface to get an accurate reading. This is checked in the same way oil level is read—on a removable dip-stick. Remove the dip-stick, wipe it clean and reinsert it for its full length. Remove and note the level of the fluid. Refill immediately if the level is low, and have the transmission checked if it drops quickly again.

There is no need to change transmission fluid any more frequently than every 30,000 miles. If the auto is used for heavy work, such as pulling a trailer, cut this time in half.

Windshield wipers. The windshield wiper is easily brought back to top condition by simply replacing the rubber blade. These are available at most service stations and in all automotive parts stores. Replacing the wiper will not do very much to preserve the life of your car, but a new blade can do a lot to save the life of the driver. How many of us have suffered with a worn wiper and have had to pull off the road in a heavy rain storm?

Tires. Tires are made in a number of different ways, each with its own special advantages. It is very important not to mix different types of tires on the same car unless a tire expert specifically recommends so. It is especially important to remember not to mix radial tires with any others on the same car. This is more of a safety point, than a device for extending the life of your car. A mixture of tires, such as radials and bias plies, could result in a steering-control loss sufficient to cause a serious accident.

Every tire has its correct inflation point. Never exceed or reduce the pressure beyond this point. When a tire is underinflated it will wear much more quickly, and cause you to use more gasoline to travel the same distance. Low tire pressure also reduces the steering capability. With power steering, it is often difficult to tell when the front-wheel tires need air, so it is important to check tire pressure regularly. (Figure 6-7.)

Figure 6-7: **Keep your tires inflated to the correct pressure. Correct inflation pressure can be found on the tire sidewall.**

An overinflated tire puts less surface on the road, and increases the possibility of skids, and also reduces steering control. Overinflation also puts a strain on the fabric and body of the tire that can shorten its life.

When tires are inconsistently inflated, you will have very little control, and the car will pull to one side or the other when stopping.

All this means that you should keep your tires inflated at *exactly* the pressure recommended by the manufacturer. And don't believe the old story about underinflation being safer in the snow and on wet roads; it just isn't so.

Tire pressure should be checked every other time you buy gasoline. Apart from replacing the small amounts of air lost over the week or two, it is also possible to spot major leaks that could turn into blow-outs if left unattended. It is important to note that **your tires will lose a pound of pressure every time the temperature** drops ten degrees. If you inflate your tires to 30 pounds in the summer at 90°, that same tire could be down to 25 pounds when the winter temperature hits 40°. That's about a 15% loss, and a serious loss of driver control.

Be sure to check the sides of the tire for cuts and serious abrasions. These can often be fixed, but they should be taken care of before they cause an accident.

Valve stems often work loose and wear out. This can be responsible for a slow loss of air. Check them out by brushing the stem with a solution of soapy water and looking for any enlarging bubbles. A warn valve stem should be replaced immediately.

The surface of your tires should be inspected every few months. Look for wear, especially abnormal wear. When tires are balanced correctly, mounted properly, and the steering components are in proper adjustment, the wear should be even. But, when you see something like excessive wear on the outside treads, you should be aware that your tires are underinflated. An overinflated tire will wear as a stripe down the middle of the tread. Unbalanced wheels will produce spotty wear and large wear spots often signify hard braking on the part of the driver.

Tires that wear normally will just gradually lose surface material until the depth of the tread is almost gone. Don't ever let the tread depth get beyond 1/16 of an inch. When tires wear to this point, it is important for road safety to replace them. (Figure 6-8.)

Figure 6-8: Never let tire-tread depth get any shallower than 1/16 of an inch. Use a quarter and place your fingernail at the edge of the coin when it bottoms in the tread. Measure the distance from your nail to the edge of the coin.

To help extend the life of your tires, it is a good idea to rotate them every 5,000 miles. This spreads the wear evenly over all the tires. It also makes your car a lot safer to drive. See the diagram for the appropriate rotation for your type of tires.

If you care for your automobile, without being a fuss-pot about it, there is, as we stated, every possibility that you can get at least 100,000 miles from it. However, the body and other outer metalwork will take a beating. Regular waxing and cleaning will make this area last. If your car does not have a protective undercoating, it is a good idea to have one put on. It can be done inexpensively, compared with the costs of other maintenance, and you should consult the dealer who sold you the car.

Driving in winter on salted roads can hasten rusting on the underside of your car. An easy way to wash off this underbody salt is to drive your car slowly, back and forth, over a lawn sprinkler.

Chapter 7

Tools:

How to use them efficiently
and make them last

It is a rare person indeed who doesn't own some tools. Rarer still, however, is the person who knows how to use and care for them properly. Good tools are an expensive investment and can save you considerable money when they are used to perform maintenance and repair chores around the home. It makes sense, therefore, that you take a little time to learn how to care for and use your tools with maximum efficiency.

Unless the tool is very simple, such as a hammer or screwdriver, it will come with some sort of instruction sheet or booklet prepared by the manufacturer. Here's a hint you'll find very effective: right now reserve some safe spot to file all these instruction sheets. It can be a file folder in your desk, a spare drawer in a kitchen cabinet, or a box in your workshop area. Collect every instruction sheet and guarantee card that you now have scattered around the house in various places. Put them all in one spot and file all future items in the same place.

When things go wrong, you'll be amazed how often the instruction booklet will tell you how to clear up the problem without an expensive trip to the repair shop. And, if the tool really needs the attention of an expert, you'll be thankful to be able to lay your hands on the guarantee or the list of authorized repair stations for the tool.

Another hint: before you invest in an expensive or specialized tool, ask yourself honestly how much use you expect to get out of it.

A snowblower can appear to be an attractive investment while you're hand shoveling the results of a snowstorm from a long driveway. However, if your area averages one blizzard every three or four years, wouldn't it be cheaper to hire some sturdy youngsters to shovel the walk?

Also, if you leave a tool unused for long periods of time, it is highly likely that maintenance will be neglected. Then, when you need it most, you may find that it isn't working at all.

Finally, consider renting specialized tools. This makes the most sense because you pay only for the use you make of it. For example, to make your trees healthy and strong, you should fertilize them every year or so by feeding the roots deep down. This means drilling holes a couple of feet deep at intervals and filling them with fertilizer. An easy way to do this job is to use an earth auger on a power drill. Rather than spend the 75 dollars or so such an outfit would cost, you can probably rent one for the day for less than ten dollars. And, if you and your neighbor share the rental time, the cost to you is only a few dollars—certainly much less expensive than investing in a tool that would be used only once a year at most.

When you finally do decide to invest in a tool, buy the best one you can afford. A good tool, whether it's a simple hand tool or a complex power tool, will save you money in the long run. A good tool works swiftly and efficiently—it saves you time and possible waste of materials. If it is a cutting tool of one sort or another, a quality tool will stay sharp longer and perform more safely. Nothing is as dangerous as a dull cutting tool.

How do you recognize a quality tool? The easiest way to make sure of quality is to ask an expert—usually your local dealer. Certain companies and brand names are associated with quality, and you'll quickly discover their names by talking to a reliable dealer.

HAND TOOLS

On these and the following pages we will cover the more common hand tools together with hints on how to use them properly to prolong their useful life.

Hammers. Because a hammer is used for banging, many people think that this tool is indestructible and treat it accordingly.

Wrong! A hammer is a carefully engineered tool that must be treated properly if you want it to last the generation of use built into it.

• If the handle is wood, make sure it is tight in the head. Wood shrinks as it dries out, and will loosen in time. The wood can be made to swell up and tighten by soaking the head and handle in water for a couple of days. Then drive the top wedges deeper, and the next day, coat the top with shellac or varnish. This protective coating will seal in the moisture and keep the handle from drying out for a long time.

• For safety, sandpaper away any rough spots or splinters on the handle and coat with shellac. If you get grease on the handle, wash it off with benzene or a similar solvent. This precaution will prevent the hammer from flying out of your hand.

• Hammer only with the face of the hammer. Don't use the cheek, or flat side, of the hammer to drive nails. A hammer head is hardened on the face to resist blows, but not on the side.

• Use a block of wood under the head of a claw hammer when removing nails. This trick lessens the stress on the head and the handle, and prevents breaking off a claw or splitting the handle.

Saws. All hand saws, whether they are crosscut, rip, keyhole, or other, require essentially the same kind of care.

• Keep your saws sharp. If you're ambitious, you can buy a saw set and a sharpening vise and file your own saws like a professional. However, a simple triangular saw file will enable you to touch-up the teeth when they show signs of dullness. You can do this several times before the saw has to go to the shop for professional attention. The effort you can save with a sharp saw is worth every minute you spend sharpening the tool.

• Keep the saws shiny and free from rust. A film of rust, besides ruining the steel, creates a lot of friction in moving through the wood and makes sawing a chore. Steel wool and some kerosene, or a commercial rust remover, will keep the blade clean (Figure 7-1).

• Store your saws carefully. In a workshop, they should be hung by the handle with nothing touching the teeth. In a toolbox, make some sort of slot in which the saws can be fitted. The important thing is to make sure that other tools don't rest on the saw and dull the teeth or bend the blade.

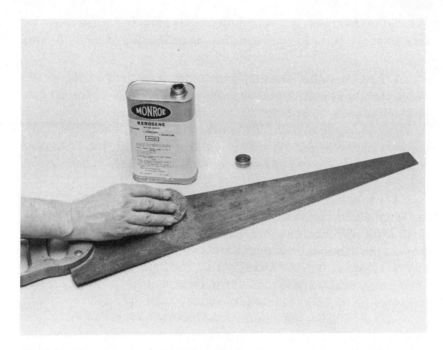

Figure 7-1:   **Kerosene and steel wool will keep your hand saws rust free and shining brightly.**

Chisels. Few tools are abused as much as chisels, with the result that their full usefulness is seldom realized.

• Chisels must be razor sharp at all times. If the edge is nicked, the tool has to be ground on a grinding wheel. Final sharpening must be done on an oilstone. If you protect the edge of the chisel from nicks, you can go for a long time without grinding.

• Never hammer the head of a chisel with a hammer. If it is necessary to use force, use a mallet, to prevent damage to the handle.

• Use a chisel only for cutting wood. Never use it as a screwdriver, a pry bar to remove lids from paint cans, or for cutting nails or other metal.

Screwdrivers. Like chisels, screwdrivers are high on the list of tools that are used improperly and quickly ruined.

• Choose the right screwdriver for the size screw. The tip should be approximately the same size as the slot in the screw head, and should fit snugly. If the tip is loose in the slot, you will either ruin the screw, mar the article being repaired, or ruin the screwdriver tip.

• The tip should be square to prevent tipping in the screw slot. Use a file to square the tip and you'll be surprised how much easier it will be to drive screws.

• Use the screwdriver only for driving or removing screws. It is not a small crowbar, a lid lifter, or a cold chisel for cutting metal.

• Don't hammer on the handle or use a wrench on the shank to increase the leverage in tightening. The only thing a screwdriver should contact is your hand at one end and a screw head at the other.

Drills. Properly speaking, a drill is the tool that holds the drill bit that revolves and makes a hole in wood or metal. Both will be covered here.

• A hand drill has a chuck that holds the drill bit, and a set of gears that turn the chuck. A light film of grease on the gear teeth, and a few drops of oil on the gear shaft and chuck, will make the tool work more easily and last longer.

• A brace looks like an oversized crank and is used with fairly large wood bits. The chuck will also take screwdriver bits if you need extra leverage on large screws. Oil the chuck to keep it from rusting. Work a few drops of oil into the ratchet mechanism that is used to lock or reverse the direction of rotation. If neglected, this part of the brace will rust tight and make the tool almost useless.

• The smaller drill bits that are used in hand and power drills are called twist drills because they resemble a twisted piece of metal. The lips at the edge of the drill do the cutting and must be kept sharp. Twist drills are usually sharpened on a grinding wheel, although there are now electric drill bit sharpeners that resemble a pencil sharpener. Look carefully at a new drill to see how the cutting edges should be sharpened.

• Cheaper twist drills are made of carbon steel. They are adequate for drilling holes in wood with a hand drill. If you intend to use the twist drill in an electric drill, or for drilling metal, buy high-speed steel bits. The extra cost will be more than amply repaid in long life and easier work.

• For drilling larger holes in wood with a brace, use an auger bit. These come in sizes up to about two inches in diameter. The secret of easy boring with these bits is to make sure the spurs on the edge of the auger are very sharp. Auger bits are not hardened like twist drills, so you can keep the edges and spurs sharp with a small file.

• Store auger bits in a special chest that holds a number of bits, in a soft cloth or plastic tool roll, or similar safe place. The idea is to keep the various bits from rubbing against each other or getting nicked by other tools.

Planes. There are many types and sizes of planes available. Usually, a nine- or ten-inch smoothing plane is the one most commonly found in home workshops. Block planes, which are smaller and used with one hand, are also very popular.

• The blade of a plane is removable and looks like a wide chisel. You should treat it as such. In other words, it must be honed on an oilstone to razor sharpness and kept that way. Avoid any situation which might nick the plane blade (Figure 7-2) and require grinding to restore the edge. When you put the plane down, always **lay it on its side. Before planing a piece of wood, make sure there are no nails that will hit the blade.**

• When planing new wood, particularly if it is resinous like pine, a gummy deposit of wood dust and resin will form on the bottom of the plane and around the cutting edges. Remove these deposits with a sponge and a solvent like turpentine. Don't use steel wool or other metal around the plane blade.

• Rub a block of paraffin on the bottom of the plane and it will glide and cut much more easily. You will put less strain on the plane and the cutting edge will last longer.

• When you put the plane away, retract the blade to prevent any nicks or damage from other tools.

Wrenches and pliers. These are similar in the sense that all are used for grasping and twisting. There are many different types and you should understand which tool is best for a particular situation if you want to do a job right and avoid breaking the tool.

• Pliers vary in the design of the jaws. Diagonal pliers are used for cutting wires; round-nose pliers are used to bend heavy wire in electrical work; needle-nosed pliers for fine work; and so on. Choose the right plier for the job you want to do. If you need help,

Figure 7-2: **Never put a plane down on its blade, particularly on a cluttered workbench. Avoid nicking the blade by laying the plane on its side all the time.**

your dealer can recommend the best design for the job you have in mind.

• For simple, all-around work in the home, the ordinary slipjoint plier is probably best. It will grasp small objects, and with a little adjustment, will open wide enough to hold most articles.

• Slipjoint pliers are best used for grasping rough round objects such as bolts. Avoid using the plier on nuts, particularly finished nuts that are found on faucets, for example. A plier will ruin the edges of the nut, and still not give you the leverage you need to tighten it properly. Use a wrench instead. A simple way to protect decorative nuts is to put a layer of cloth or masking tape between the nut and the wrench. Tape can be stuck right to the face of the wrench jaws.

• Keep the joint oiled to prevent the pin from rusting and making it difficult to use the plier.

• Wrenches come in various designs. Each is basically adjustable, or fixed, in size. Adjustable wrenches take more time to use because you have to constantly adjust the jaws for the size of nut you are working on. They offer the convenience of simplicity—a single wrench will handle a wide range of sizes. A fixed wrench, such as the familiar box or open-end wrench that you see sticking out of the pocket of your neighborhood mechanic, will work much more quickly when used on the right-sized bolt or nut. To be ready for various repair jobs, however, means that you have to own a full range of sizes—no small investment.

• Nothing will damage a nut or a wrench more quickly than using a wrench that is a size too big. The nut will wedge against the corners of the wrench and both will be ruined.

• The sockets of socket wrenches should be kept clean with a lightly-oiled rag. This will keep the locking pin working smoothly, so changing sockets will be an easy job.

• When using a wrench on chromium-plated nuts, first put layers of adhesive tape on the jaws. This will prevent scratching or marring finished surfaces.

Measuring tools. These come in such forms as tapes or rules. To maintain accuracy, remember these points:

• A measuring tool is useless unless it measures accurately. With straight rules, accuracy is affected by end wear. This is particularly apt to happen with wooden rules such as yardsticks. Be careful that the ends are not damaged when you use the rule. With steel tapes, avoid pulling the tape too tight when you're measuring lengths. The strain on the tape may bend the end hook and in effect "stretch" the rule.

• Keep steel tapes clean. Any grit on the tape will cause the gradations to wear as you pull the tape back and forth in its case. Wipe the entire tape length with a soft cloth that is lightly oiled to keep it working smoothly for a long time. (Figure 7-3.)

• On folding rules, keep the joints lightly oiled. In addition to prolonging the useful life of the rule, this simple step will make it much easier to use.

• Most rules are also used as straightedges. Avoid nicking the edges, and destroying their accuracy, by keeping sharp or heavy objects away from them. The best way to store rules is to lay them

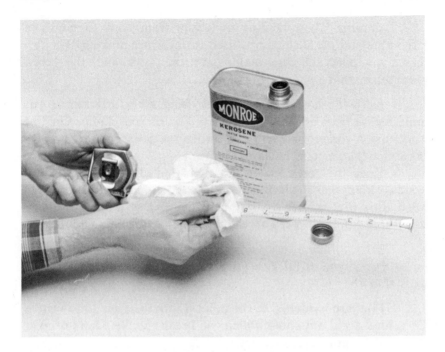

Figure 7-3: **Kerosene and a soft rag are all you need to keep a steel tape working smoothly and accurately for years.**

flat on narrow shelves to prevent them from bending. Long rules have a hole for hanging which should be used.

Checking tools. Included under this heading are such tools as try squares, combination squares, bevel protractors, levels, and the like.

• Treat every square and level as delicate instruments, and never use them as improvised tools to do anything other than to check the accuracy of your work.

• Never lay a square down where another tool can be placed on top of it. Even a slight weight on the blade can affect its accuracy.

• Protractors, bevels, and other tools that have moving parts should be kept clean and well-oiled. If possible, keep all such tools in protective cases or the boxes in which they were purchased. This is particularly important if you use such tools on the job, and you have to carry them in a tool box.

Clamps. These holding tools vary from small C-clamps to large pipe and parallel clamps used in furniture making. The two important parts of any clamp are the jaws and the screw mechanism that operates the clamp.

• Keep the jaws clean and free from nicks and burrs. Any imperfection will be impressed on the work you clamp. On fine work, use a piece of scrap wood under the jaws of the clamp to prevent damage to a finished surface.

• Keep the screw clean and lightly oiled. When using in a woodworking shop, clamp screws are apt to collect a coating of wood dust that makes operation difficult. Use a toothbrush or something similar to keep threads clean and free of clogging dust.

Files. Files are very useful tools for a variety of shaping jobs on both wood and metal. Few people treat them like the fine cutting tools that they are.

• Files are hardened to the point where they are quite brittle. Therefore, avoid any shock which can break the file. Don't drop or throw files onto hard surfaces.

• Files cut best when they are clean. Don't clean a file by rapping it against the side of a bench; a file-cleaning brush is both cheap and efficient.

• Always use a handle on the end of a file. It will be easier to use, and to control the cutting action. It will also prevent a nasty puncture wound in the palm if the file slips.

• When filing soft metals, such as aluminum or copper, the chips often stick in the teeth and cause marks on the filed surface. You can prevent this by rubbing ordinary blackboard chalk on the teeth before you file such materials.

Sandpaper. Most people use the term "sandpaper" for any kind of paper coated with an abrasive. Actually, there are several different types and each should be chosen for a particular application.

• Old-fashioned sandpaper is really flint paper. It is cheap but wears very rapidly. If you have a messy sanding job that will clog sandpaper—such as sanding old painted surfaces—use this paper. This paper will clog like any other type you might use, but it can be replaced often without spending too much money. Wiping the sandpaper with some turpentine on a sponge or brush will help you get a bit more use from the sheet before you have to throw it away.

• Garnet paper is fairly cheap and is good for finish sanding of new wood surfaces. Some old-time furniture makers swear by it, but it is being replaced by synthetic abrasives.

• Aluminum oxide paper is made with synthetic abrasive grains. It is extremely tough and durable, and while more expensive than flint or garnet paper, it will last a long time sanding a variety of materials. In the long run, it is probably your most economical abrasive paper.

• Silicon carbide paper is another synthetic abrasive that is even harder than aluminum oxide. It is one of the hardest known materials and is useful for smoothing such materials as glass, ceramics, tiles, and hard metals.

• Emery paper or cloth is used on metals. Like the flint papers, emery is quickly dulled by use. Aluminum oxide or silicon carbide paper is now preferred for finishing the surfaces of metals.

• Any abrasive paper will last longer and do a better job if it is used wrapped around a flat block of wood. This spreads the work and the wear over a greater surface area.

• Lift the sandpaper block off the work often while sanding and also rap off the accumulated dust. This will extend the life of the sheet of abrasive and make it cut much more efficiently.

Soldering irons. Most soldering irons used by amateur workers are heated electrically. Basically there are two types: a quick-heating soldering gun, and a soldering iron that takes a minute or two to warm up.

• A soldering gun is useful for heavy work. In fact, it often comes with different tips that enable you to soften and cut composition tile and plastics. Don't use this type of iron for fine electrical work, like repairing your hi-fi.

• A small soldering iron (from 25 to 40 watts) is your best bet for soldering fine electrical components.

• File the tip to the desired shape with a smooth file. As you use the iron, keep cleaning the tip by rubbing it across a lightly-moistened sponge. This will keep the tip bright and your soldering will go very easily. If the tip oxidizes, heat will not pass efficiently to your work. Then it is time to file the tip again.

Oilstones. While not a tool in itself, an oilstone is a very important adjunct to your toolbox and you should know how to use and maintain the cutting action.

• Oilstones come in various grits (degrees of smoothness of grains). The most useful one is about two by six inches with a fine grit on one side and a coarser grit on the other. This type will enable you to sharpen virtually every tool you own.

• Oilstones should not be used dry; soak them with thin oil before using. Keep a film of oil on the surface as you use the stone.

• Keep the oilstone in a dustfree box between uses. Ordinary dust, when combined with the oil on the surface of the stone, forms a gummy film which reduces the cutting action.

• If the stone is gummed up, clean it with kerosene and then oil the surface.

• When sharpening tools, try to use the entire surface of the stone. This will equalize wear and keep the stone relatively flat. If you keep rubbing a tool in one area, you will wear a groove or depression in the stone and make it useless for honing a fairly large flat blade like a plane iron.

SMALL POWER TOOLS

Small power tools include drills, sanders, circular and saber saws, and similar portable tools. Wisely chosen, these tools can save you a lot of work in doing both routine and specialized jobs. Keeping them in shape and ready to work for you is really a simple matter if you observe the following pointers.

With small electric tools it is even more important that you buy the best quality tool you can afford. If you buy a cheap screwdriver and it breaks, the most you will lose is the price of the tool. If you buy a cheap drill and the insulation around the motor is defective, you can get a nasty shock. The lesson is obvious.

The main reason for the varying prices of similar tools, apart from general differences in quality, is the power rating of the motor and the type of bearings provided. Low-priced tools usually have very small motors and simple sleeve bearings. Such a tool is adequate for occasional light-duty work. If the tool is run continuously, or under a heavy load, the motor will overheat and burn out. A tool with a heavy-duty motor and ball bearings will work for long periods of time without developing serious problems.

You should consider getting a heavy-duty tool if you expect to do a fair amount of work, or if you intend adding accessories. Even a light-duty electric drill will handle a variety of small drilling jobs in wood without problems. However, if you try adding an accessory such as a sanding disc, a grinder, or a buffing wheel, you may find that the drill simply will not run these accessories without overheating. Therefore, the first step in getting long life and value out of every power tool you own or consider purchasing, is to know its limitations and use it accordingly.

Any power tool you buy should be protected against shock. Some tools have grounded, three-prong plugs. Don't bypass this safety feature by cutting off the grounding prong, or neglecting to use the plug with a proper adaptor if you do not have three-pronged outlets where you work. Newer tools are designed with double insulation which eliminates the need for the grounding plug. The precaution to keep in mind here is that you should not tamper with the tool beyond routine maintenance recommended by the tool manufacturer. If you do, you may short-circuit the double insulation design provisions and make the tool dangerous for use.

Finally, be careful with extension cords. Most power tools will need an extension cord at times and you should use one adequate to carry the current needed to operate the tool efficiently. Usually, this information comes with the tool. A heavy-duty tool will not operate properly if you plug it into a light extension cord.

Electric drills. The most popular electric drill for the average homeowner is either a 1/4 inch or 3/8 inch drill. Consider spending somewhat more and get a drill that has a reversible, variable-speed feature. It makes drilling in a variety of materials easier. The size refers to the diameter drill bit that can be used in the chuck. The smaller the drill, the faster it revolves. Because of their higher speed, the smaller drills are good with sanding or grinding accessories that need high speeds. A larger drill, like a 1/2 inch drill, revolves too slowly for sanding but will drill large holes in concrete, heavy timbers, and the like.

• Every drill requires periodic lubrication and replacement of brushes. Oil holes are usually conspicuous and should receive a drop or two of light oil every couple of hours. The gears inside the drill housing are packed in grease which should be cleaned out and replaced according to the manufacturer's recommendations.

• Depending on the particular design of the tool, replacement of brushes can be easy or difficult. If you are given a choice between two drills of identical quality, choose the one where brush replacement is easy. If the brushes are concealed inside the tool, you may have the extra expense of sending the tool back to the manufacturer or repair shop every time you want to replace the motor brushes.

• If the drill gets uncomfortably hot in your hand, you can be sure you are overloading it. Ease up on the pressure, stop it frequently for cooling, or do both.

• Remember that every accessory for an electric drill (and there are too many to mention) is a compromise of one sort or another. For example, a sanding disc on the end of a drill will not work as efficiently as a regular disc sander. Drill accessories are useful for occasional jobs. If you find yourself constantly using a certain accessory, you should consider getting a separate tool to do the job.

Circular electric saws. Next to a hammer this is probably the most useful tool a carpenter can own. This saw is usually used for sawing construction lumber—studs, joists, planking and the like. Consider purchasing this saw if you intend to do remodeling or new construction. If you expect to do finer paneling or trim work, the smaller circular trim saw, or a saber saw, might be a better choice. For minimum construction work, the saw should be able to cut through a two-inch thick piece of lumber when the blade is set at a 45-degree angle. This means at least a seven or seven- and one-half inch diameter blade.

• Before using a circular saw, make sure the work is firmly supported. If the work is not supported adequately, you are inviting an accident that can hurt either you or the saw.

• A circular saw works best and safest when the blade is sharp. A dull blade strains the saw, overloads the motor, and tires the operator.

• Keep the bottom of the saw free of gummy residue. Ordinary turpentine will clean resinous wood dust from metal parts. Paint thinner can also be used; it's a lot less expensive than turpentine. A little wax rubbed on the bottom and rubbing edges will make the saw glide easily on the work.

• Before starting the saw, make sure the blade will not touch anything except the wood you're cutting. Be especially careful that you don't cut the electric cord.

• Choose the right blade for the job you're doing. A combination blade is suitable for general cutting. However, if you expect to rip long boards, you'll do it faster and easier if you use a regular ripping blade. Specialized blades, such as a hollow-ground or plywood blade, should only be used for the purpose designed.

• The lower blade guard should retract easily as the saw enters the work and then spring back quickly at the end of the cut. If it doesn't, the reason is that sawdust is gumming the bearings of the guard. Clean with turpentine and then oil lightly.

• Some saws are permanently lubricated; others require periodic lubrication. Check the manufacturer's instruction on this point. Brushes have to be replaced at intervals. The comments made under electric drills apply here.

• Make sure that the saw blade does not bind in long cuts. This is particularly apt to happen when cutting a large sheet of plywood or a long board. A sudden binding of the blade can damage the blade or the saw at the very least. Even more serious is the potential for a serious accident if you lose control of the saw.

Saber or jig saw. For the amateur worker, this is probably the handiest saw to own because it can cut straight or along a curve. It is light and more easily handled than a circular saw, and a variety of blades are available for cutting lumber, plywood and metals.

• Use sharp blades to prevent overloading the motor. Generally, it is impractical to sharpen the easily replaceable blades, although you can "touch-up" the teeth lightly with a small file to get some extra life from them.

• Observe the manufacturer's recommendations on oiling. After using the saw, fine sawdust will accumulate in crevices. Use a small, stiff paintbrush to clean the saw often (Figure 7-4). If your vacuum cleaner converts to a blower, use that.

Power sanders. There are several different types which use sheets, belts, or discs for sanding both wood and metal. Getting the most out of a sander first means choosing the right machine for the job at hand.

Figure 7-4:   An ordinary paintbrush is an ideal tool for cleaning
sawdust out of hard-to-get-at-places on power tools.

• The most popular sander for home use is either the orbital
or the oscillating sander. These machines usually use a piece of
sandpaper about 3 by 7 inches which cuts without waste from a
standard sheet of abrasive. The orbital sander has a motor which
drives the sanding pad in an orbital motion, and makes small
circles on the work surface. Some have a switch or lever which
enables you to convert the action to straight line sanding which is
better for the finish sanding operation. Oscillating sanders are
economical because they have a simple vibrating mechanism which
moves the sanding pad in a rapid, short motion. Both orbital and
oscillating sanders should be considered to be finish sanders.

Neither is powerful enough to remove any great quantity of material, such as is needed when refinishing a worn spot on a hardwood floor.

- A belt sander will remove a lot of material very quickly. It should not be used for finish sanding on furniture. For large surfaces, such as a boat deck, it is the ideal choice. The most popular sizes take belts either three or four inches in width. For home use, a three-inch belt sander would be the best choice.

- A portable disc sander is another fast-acting abrasive tool. Most owners of small drills eventually buy a disc sanding attachment and use it with indifferent results. A disc sander, whether you buy it as an attachment to your drill, or as a separate tool, takes some practice use on wood to prevent deep swirl marks. A disc sander is good for removing coats of paint before repainting if a belt sander is not available or if paint remover is impractical. The heavy-duty disc sander finds most use in auto body shops where it is ideal for smoothing patches and imperfections in body repairs.

- Any sander will work faster, and the abrasive paper will last longer, if you use a light touch. Generally speaking, the weight of the machine is all the pressure that should be exerted on the work surface. Bearing down hard on the sander will not make it cut faster; it will simply increase friction, overwork the motor, and clog the abrasive paper.

- Lift the sander frequently and brush or blow away the accumulated sawdust. At the same time shake off the excess sawdust from the sanding pad. If possible, try to buy a sander that has a vacuum-type dust collector. This is especially handy with a belt sander which throws up a lot of sawdust.

- On a belt sander, check the alignment of the sanding belt frequently as you work. The sander has an adjusting knob that enables you to adjust the tension on the belt very easily, and keep the edge of the belt from running off and cutting into the housing of the machine (Figure 7-5).

- Use the right abrasive for the job. For quick stock removal, start with a coarse grit, and then work your way down to a fine grit. Trying to do the whole job with a fine grit will simply wear out the abrasive quicker. On messy, gummy work—like removing old paint—use an open-coat abrasive. This means the grains are paced far apart to prevent clogging of the surface.

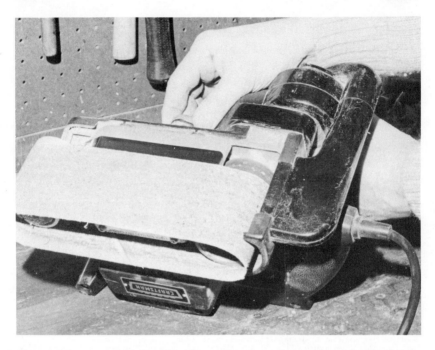

Figure 7-5:   **On a belt sander, make sure the belt is centered and running true. Otherwise, you run the risk of cutting into the housing of the tool.**

• An inexpensive dust mask is a worthwhile investment in comfort when sanding. Also, if you intend to sand overhead, a pair of goggles should be part of your equipment.

Router. At one time the router was a specialized tool for professional carpenters. Now it is being found increasingly in amateur workshops because it is so handy for a variety of cutting jobs. Here's how to get the most out of your router:

• The power of routers ranges from one-quarter to one horsepower. The small ones are suitable for occasional, light-duty work. If you expect to do much work, you should certainly consider getting one of the more powerful models.

• The router bit spins at about 20,000 rpm. At this speed, the bit will quickly burn the work and possibly overheat to the point of losing temper, unless you keep it moving in the work. On the other hand, too hard a feed will also overload the machine. This is the one power tool that requires a bit of practice before you can use it on finished work.

• Heavy or deep cuts should be handled in stages. This will make both machine and bit last longer, and give you a better-looking job.

STATIONARY POWER TOOLS

These are the larger tools, such as circular saws, that are used in a fixed place. Many of the previous comments regarding small power tools also apply to larger power tools.

Circular saws. The ordinary table saw uses a blade eight to ten inches in diameter. Various attachments are available to increase the scope of work you can handle, but they should not be used until you feel perfectly at home with the ordinary routines of crosscutting and ripping.

• Above all, make sure the blade is sharp. Even a slightly dull blade can overload the machine and invite accidents. You are tempted to push the work harder into the blade, thereby increasing your chances of slipping into the blade.

• Use the right blade for the work at hand. A combination blade is adequate for general crosscutting or ripping, provided you don't push too much. If you have a number of 2 by 4's that you want to rip into 2 by 2's, you should replace the blade with a regular ripping blade. A fine-toothed plywood blade will give you a nice cut on plywood, but will quickly dull and burn your work if you use it for general cutting.

• Keep the table clean of scraps of wood and accumulated sawdust. Keep a dust brush handy to clean out the slots in the table so that the miter gage and rip fence will move easily.

• Wax the surface of the table with automobile paste wax. This will make it easier to push the work into the blade and prevent the accumulation of moisture-absorbing sawdust and attendant rust problems.

Radial-arm saws. This saw does much the same work as the bench saw, except that all cutting is done from the top rather than from below as with the table saw.

- Table life can be increased if you install a thin plywood sheet on top of the working table. When that gets cut and scored, simply replace the sheet with a new one.

- Every radial-arm saw has a number of adjustments to maintain squareness and alignment in cutting operations. Check the alignment of the saw frequently according to the manufacturer's instructions. A blade that is not properly aligned will bind in the saw cut, increase the load on the machine, and get dull quickly.

- The motor and the blade are held in a unit called the yoke which travels on guide rails under the arm of the saw. Keep these rails clean of sawdust. If not kept clean, they will gum up in time, and pulling the blade through the work will become difficult. The accuracy of your work will suffer.

- Sawdust and oil mix to form a gum. Therefore, any lubrication of woodworking machinery like the radial-arm saw should be done with a greaseless lubricant. A bar of kitchen paraffin is very useful to rub along slides and other moving parts.

Drill press. After a power saw, this is usually the next most useful tool you can add to your workshop. With proper accessories, the drill press can drill, rout, sand, wire brush metal, and even drill square holes with a special mortising bit.

- Raise the adjustable table up as close as possible to find the chuck when you drill wood or metal. The more you have to pull down the feed lever before contacting the work, the more wear you put on the bearings, especially if you use a tool with an off center of gravity, like a fly cutter.

- Protect the adjustable table with a piece of wood if you are drilling completely through a piece of work. Also, make sure the drill bit is centered over the hole in the table.

- When drilling, make sure the work is held firmly in a drill-press vise or is clamped securely to the table. If the work is hand held, it may be pulled out of your hand causing both injury and damage. (Figure 7-6.)

- When drilling metal, the drill bit can jam in the hole at the moment it breaks through the other side of the piece. Develop a feel for that moment and keep the drill from cutting through too rapidly. This will save a lot of broken drill bits.

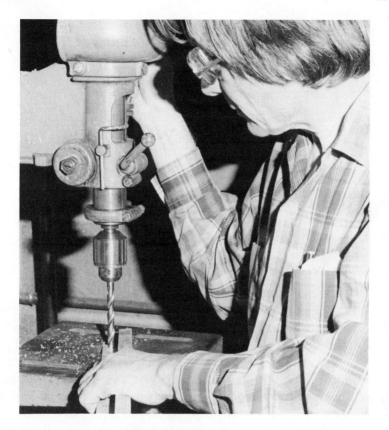

Figure 7-6: **Never hold a workpiece with your hand when using a drill press. You may damage your workpiece, break the drill bit, or hurt yourself.**

Band saw. A continuous steel blade, in the form of an endless loop running around two wheels, is the basic principle of a band saw. It is useful for cutting curves in heavy wood and for making cuts in thick timbers.

• Blades come in various widths; the narrower the width, the smaller the radius you can cut. Trouble comes when you try to cut too tight a circle with too wide a blade. The blade is twisted, burns the wood, and puts excess load on the motor. Don't be afraid to change blades for different kinds of jobs.

• The blade guide should be adjusted so that it just clears the top of the work you're cutting. If you neglect this adjustment and cut various thicknesses of work with a length of unsupported blade, you will find it difficult to follow a cutting line. In addition, you will be putting extra wear on the blade guides.

Jig saw. The stationary jig saw, also called a scroll saw, is useful for making more intricate cuts than is possible with the band saw.

• The comment regarding blade width made above also applies to the jig saw. The more intricate the cut, the narrower the blade choice.

• Remember that the saw cuts with a reciprocating action, cutting on the downstroke only. Therefore, if you press the work too hard into the blade, you increase friction on the blade on the up-stroke that doesn't cut.

• The lighter the touch, the longer your blade will last.

Bench grinder. The usual bench grinder consists of a motor with a grinding wheel on each end of the motor shaft. One wheel is generally of medium grit while the other is finer for finish grinding.

• When replacing wheels make sure you buy a grindstone that is rated for the speed of your grinder. If you run a wheel at a speed higher than recommended, you run the serious risk that the wheel will disintegrate under centrifugal force and cause serious injury.

• Invest in a wheel-dressing tool (Figure 7-7). There are several types that are fairly inexpensive, and it will help you keep the wheel cutting freely and accurately.

• Most grinders have sealed ball bearings that need no lubrication. However, if there are oil or grease cups on the machine, lubricate the grinder according to manufacturer's recommendations.

Other power tools. Other tools such as jointers, lathes, shapers, and belt sanders are frequently part of an amateur's workshop.

• Because features vary among various machines, it is possible only to give general suggestions for increasing their life and usefulness. Therefore, the first step is to read all the instructions provided by the manufacturer.

Figure 7-7: A wheel-dressing tool is a good investment. By keeping the wheels free from clogging, you will find that they cut faster and last longer.

• Keep your machine clean. A shop vacuum is almost a necessity if you have several power tools. A clean machine works easier, and you can see what you're doing much more easily.

• Most power tools have large surfaces of cast iron or steel. These will rust if not protected. Oil can't be used because it combines with sawdust to form a gummy mess. A hard paste wax will not only protect surfaces from rust, it will also make work pieces slide more smoothly.

To get the most from all your tools, whether they are hand tools, portable tools, or stationary power tools, observe these simple rules:

• When you need a tool, you should be able to find it quickly. In other words, make some provision for storing your tools properly, and always return them to their proper places when finished. You'll be amazed how quickly a Saturday-morning repair chore will be completed when you can put your hands on the exact tool you seek.

• Always read and save in a permanent place all the manufacturer's literature that comes with the tool. The simple precaution of reading directions *first* can prolong the life of your tools and keep you from hurting yourself.

• Keep your tools in good repair. If it is a cutting tool, keep blades and cutters as sharp as possible. A sharp tool always works faster and with less strain on man and machine.

Following these common-sense rules should make it easy for you to get two and three times more use and enjoyment from all your tools.

Chapter 8

Garden Tools and Equipment:

How to get extra growing seasons from your investment.

Garden tools and equipment are probably subjected to more abuse than any other things you own. Part of this abuse comes from the nature of the work with hard soils, heavy rocks, and tough plant materials. Because the work is sometimes rough, it is easy to forget the simple maintenance techniques that you would take for granted on an indoor tool.

Hand tools and manually-operated equipment will be covered in this chapter. Equipment using small gasoline and electric motors, such as lawn mowers and the like, will be treated in the next chapter.

BUYING TOOLS FOR LONG LIFE

How long a tool will last depends a lot on how well you choose it in the first place. This means more than buying quality, although that is very important for long life. It also means choosing the right tool for the particular purpose you have in mind. Let's take a simple shovel as an example:

Do you know that there are two basic types of shovel, and that most gardeners buy the wrong one for the purpose they have in mind? Shovels can be classed as *digging* shovels or *loading* shovels. The difference is in the angle the handle makes with the blade or scoop. A shovel used for digging is called a spade; it is relatively straight from the handle to the blade. For loading things, such as coal or grain, you use a shovel. It is somewhat more bent than a spade, the scoop making more of an angle with the handle. Yet, many people will use the wrong shovel for the job and wonder why they get backaches. More about this later.

Here are pointers that are general in nature and apply to many types of outdoor work implements:

• Look at the thickness of metal used to make the tool. Generally speaking, the thicker the steel, the longer the life you can expect.

• Common sense, or a knowledgeable salesperson, will indicate where the greatest strain occurs during use of the tool. Is the tool reinforced at areas of great stress? A spade used for digging should have, for example, an extra heavy lip attached to the back of the blade so you can really bear down on the blade with your heel when sinking it into the earth.

• What about rust? Is the tool plated in some way to minimize corrosion? A tool will last a long time if it is easy to clean with no hidden crevices that can collect dirt and water.

• Is the handle smooth and comfortable to use? If a tool is awkward to hold or handle, you will probably use it improperly and reduce its life.

• Is the tool easy to hang up out of the way? Almost any tool with a wooden handle can be made more convenient if you drill a hole in the end so you can hang it on a pegboard hook or smooth nail.

• On cutting tools, check the problems involved in keeping the tool sharp. Are blades readily replaceable, or must they be resharpened? If resharpening is the only way, can you do it yourself with a file or a grindstone, or is this something that will have to be returned to a service shop?

• Finally, on small hand tools choose bright colors if at all possible. This makes it easy to see the tools on the grass, and is a great safety aid. There is less risk of running over a tool with a lawn mower if it stands out. Your current stock of tools may be sprayed a bright color on the handles for visibility. In addition, this distinctive color will identify your tools when they are "borrowed" by friends.

SHOVELING AND DIGGING TOOLS

Shovels. This is a *loading* tool and should not be used for digging. The angle between the handle and the scoop is more than that for a spade. A long-handled shovel gives you greater leverage when lifting the load.

- Try several before you buy, and get one that is the right size for your height. Lay the bottom of the scoop flat on the ground. With your hand resting naturally at your side, the end of the handle should come to your palm, with the bottom of the scoop staying flat on the ground. If the scoop lifts off the ground, the handle is too short. If there is still handle left when it is even with your palm, the handle is too long.
- Make sure the scoop is so designed that metal comes up the handle for some distance and reinforces it.
- A round end will cut into a pile of material more easily than a square end.
- Don't use a shovel for loosening or lifting heavy rocks.
- Wipe with an oily rag and hang up each time after using.

Spades. This is a *digging* tool and is straighter than a loading shovel. If you use it as a loading shovel, you will find yourself bending over more than necessary and putting a strain on your back. When you hold the spade with the handle vertical, your foot should rest naturally on the lip on the back of the blade so you can bring the full force from your hip for loosening the soil. In other words, a spade is less bent than a shovel.

- A shorter D-handle spade is easier to use than one with a long handle, and causes less strain on the blade.
- The blade should come up the handle for some distance for reinforcement. A square-end blade is handy for cutting roots and transplanting.
- The lip on the back of the spade should be substantial. Avoid a simple rolled edge.
- Use care in levering rocks and stones loose when digging a hole. It takes a strong tool to withstand this kind of strain. Use a crowbar instead.
- Use a file to keep the edge of the blade sharp (Figure 8-1).
- Wipe with an oily rag and hang up after each use.

Spading fork. This is used for loosening and turning soil before planting.

- Look for the same kind of construction that was suggested above for spades.

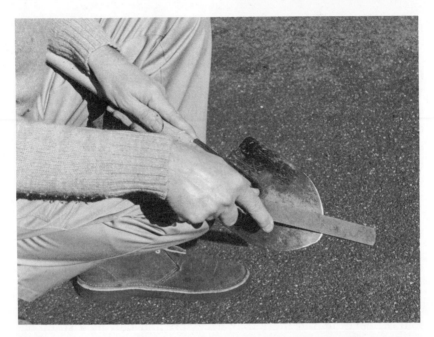

Figure 8-1:   **An ordinary file will keep garden tools sharp and working better. You'll also save your back.**

• Avoid loosening heavy stones with a fork—the tines simply cannot do the job without bending permanently.

• A long-handled fork is useful to a farmer who is tossing hay above his head. A suburban-type gardener should get a shorter fork with an easy-to-hold handle shaped like the letter "D".

Trowel. This is strictly a "hands-and-knees" tool and should be used for light work.

• If you hit a stone bigger than a baseball, get a bigger digging tool to remove it. It is very easy to put a permanent kink in the end of a trowel.

• A trowel made out of forged steel is usually easier to use and more long-lasting than one made out of thin, pressed steel.

• Wipe carefully before storing away.

RAKING TOOLS

Iron rake. This is the tool to reach for after you've spaded or forked an area prior to planting.

• The inexpensive flat iron rake with short straight teeth should be used for light-duty work. Don't use it if you're going to rake out a lot of stone much bigger than golf balls.

• For heavier work, get a bow rake with curved teeth. A metal bow attached at each end of the rake is fastened to the rake handle some distance above the rake itself. It has more spring and won't bend if you move larger stones.

• Save your back and your rake by making a small pile of stones and then scooping them up into a wheelbarrow. Don't try to rake everything to the edge of your property.

• Don't use the corner of the rake to pry out larger stones; you're sure to bend the end teeth, or possibly break the rake right off the handle.

• For safety's sake, hang up the rake after you're finished. Stepping on a rake can put a tine through your foot or give you a nasty blow on the head when the handle swings up. It's funny in a slapstick movie, but can be quite dangerous in real life.

Lawn rakes. These are really brooms and are made of light strips of springy steel or bamboo.

• Don't use either of these rakes for smoothing freshly-dug earth. The teeth will not take such treatment.

• Use these rakes with a light sweeping motion to clean up grass clippings or leaves.

• After each use, clean the teeth of debris. Using the rake upside down for a few strokes will remove accumulated leaves or grass. A rag lightly oiled with linseed oil is the best maintenance tool.

CUTTING TOOLS

A variety of different cutting tools are used outdoors on trees, shrubbery, and grass. Each requires a little care in use to get the best service.

Pruning saws. These come in various styles and sizes. Choose the one that best fits the requirements you have in mind. A pruning saw is the only tool to use if you want to cut a branch or stalk an inch or more in diameter.

• Keep the saw sharp with a small triangular file.

- After each use, wipe the blade with an oily rag to prevent the sap from rusting the blade. Remove all shreds of sawdust from between the teeth with the rag.

Long-handled loppers. These are used on smaller branches, less than an inch in diameter.

- Don't try to cut branches larger than one inch. The strain on the handles will be too much.
- If the handles bend, the blade may be dull or the branch too big. Sharpen the blade or use a pruning saw.
- Keep the blade sharp with a flat file or oilstone.
- Wipe after each use to prevent rust. A drop of oil on the pivot will also make the tool easier to use and longer lasting.

Pruning shears. These come in two models and are used mostly for pruning thinner stalks on shrubbery. They are difficult to use if you try to cut something much over a quarter of an inch in diameter. One style looks like a pair of pliers with cutting blades similar to a scissor. The other style has a single cutting blade that presses down on a soft metal anvil. This type makes neat clean cuts, especially useful in flower arranging.

- On either model, keep the blade sharp. With the anvil type of pruning shear, make sure that in sharpening you preserve the relationship between the edge of the blade and the anvil. The blade has to touch the anvil along its whole length at the same instant, otherwise you will not be able to completely cut through a stalk.
- Keep the tool oiled and cleaned. Never put away a pruning shear without first wiping it carefully. Once you have a bit of rust on the blade or in the pivot, you've lost the best part of its use.

Pruning knife. This is used for light cuttings. The only maintenance required here is to keep it sharp and free from moisture. Remember—the sharper the blade, the safer the knife. Accidents happen when you try to force a dull blade to do work.

Grass shears and clippers. These are really heavy duty scissors and are used for trimming grass along beds where a mower can't reach.

- Use grass shears only for clipping grass. They are not to be used for pruning, however small the job may seem.

• Most grass shears have a compound lever system and a spring to keep the blades apart. The slightest bit of rust here will make the shears difficult to use. Keep the shears well oiled and wiped dry after each use.

• Keep the blades well sharpened and free from nicks.

Hedge clippers. These are really giant scissors and should be handled as such.

• Cut as close as possible to the pivot near the handles. This keeps strain on the handles at a minimum and makes your work easier.

• Keep the blades sharp and the pivot well oiled to preserve easy-working action at all times.

• Because of the nature of the work, the blades will rust quickly unless you keep wiping them with an oily rag. Rust will cut down cutting efficiency. You can, however, remove the rust and built-up accumulation of dried sap with some steel wool and kerosene.

Lawn edgers and ice chippers. Don't get these two tools confused or try to use one to do the other's job.

• A lawn edger has a rounded blade and a lip for your heel to press down on. Keep the edge sharp with a file.

• An ice chipper has a straight blade that is much heavier than an edger. Use it with short, stabbing strokes to break up areas of ice.

• Because of the work they do, they should always be dried. Also, neither tool should be used with a prying action.

CHOPPING AND CULTIVATING TOOLS

• A long-handled hoe is used to cut weeds slightly below the surface of the ground. Use it with a slicing action towards you; don't push large mounds of earth around with the blade as if it were a miniature bulldozer.

• A sharp hoe makes for easy work. A file is the easiest way of keeping it sharp, even while you're working in the field.

• A pronged cultivator should only be used on light weeds, ones that can be easily pulled up with the fingers of the tool.

• Look carefully at small hand tools before you buy them. Many are entirely too flimsy, even for the light jobs they are intended to do. Spending twice as much on a tool can often mean more than twice the life.

OTHER TYPES OF GARDEN EQUIPMENT

Before you buy something specialized, make sure you have a continuing need for the article. Too often a gardener gets caught up in gadgetry with the result that after one or two uses, the tool languishes in the garage gathering rust. A post-hole digger is a good example of such a tool. It is usually wiser to rent such an implement.

Hoses and sprinklers. No garden can depend entirely on rain. You have to have some sort of arrangement for watering lawns and plants artificially.

• Hoses are made of rubber or plastic and will last a long time with proper care. Rubber lasts longest, is heavier, and is much more expensive. Plastic is a joy to lift, but you have to realize that its life is shorter.

• Every hose will last longer if it is rolled up on a reel or hanger after each use. Don't let a hose lie for days in the hot sun, or out in freezing weather.

• If you have high water pressure, the life of your hose will be shortened if you use the nozzle as a shutoff device. In such a case, shut the water at the faucets.

• Try not to drag hoses where they will be abraded by rough concrete or caught on sharp rocks. (Figure 8-2.) Avoid kinks and sharp bends, and riding over them with any vehicle.

• When storing hoses for the winter, make sure they are thoroughly drained. If water freezes inside, it might split the hose.

• Rinse out metal sprinkling cans thoroughly after using any sort of fertilizer or plant feeding solution. Most of these chemicals are corrosive to metal.

Fertilizer spreader. Most spreaders work well the first year, but are useless the next season because the owner neglected a simple maintenance chore.

Figure 8-2: **Avoid letting your hose get kinked around sharp objects. This is an easy way to shorten its life.**

• After *every use,* clean the spreader thoroughly to get rid of every trace of fertilizer from around the teeth and feed holes. Most fertilizers are corrosive and will quickly ruin a spreader if the tool is put away in anything but an absolutely clean condition.

• Moving parts should get regular lubrication to keep them easy working and the gauging system feeding accurately.

• Each manufacturer has designed his spreader to distribute the fertilizer at a predetermined rate. Don't tamper with any parts other than the adjustments.

Garden sprayer. Many of the same comments made about fertilizer spreaders apply here also.

• After *every use,* clean the sprayer thoroughly to get rid of the particular solution you may have used. Clean the hose and nozzle well, in addition to the outside of the unit.

• If your unit has a leather plunger that is used to build up pressure in the tank, that should be kept oiled to prevent the leather from drying out.

Wheelbarrows and garden carts. These are great helps in moving material from one part of your yard to another.

• You will prolong the life of any unit by keeping it clean. Hose out the pan or cart whenever you carry things like fertilizer, lime or cement.

• Make sure you oil axles and wheel bearings to make the unit easy to move. If you have pneumatic tires, make sure they are inflated to the recommended pressures. A soft tire is hard to push, while a hard, overinflated tire will wear quickly.

• Most damage is caused by overloading. If you want to carry heavy cinder blocks or bags of cement, invest in a heavy-duty contractor's wheelbarrow. Don't expect a light garden-type wheelbarrow to take such a load. Or, break up the load and make twice as many trips.

• Wood parts should be wiped with a linseed-oil soaked rag. The same rag can be used to wipe unprotected metal parts to prevent rust. If you neglect this treatment, the pan of a metal wheelbarrow will quickly rust, and on light duty models, a hole will soon rust through and destroy the usefulness of the equipment.

• Units with pneumatic tires should not be stored for long periods of time or between seasons with the tires resting on the ground or concrete. They may develop a flat spot. Either store the unit up on short blocks under the axle or hang it on a wall.

Lawn mowers.

• A hand mower can be very easy to use if it is kept sharp and free from rust. After each use, wipe off the blades with an oily rag. If you notice any nicks on the blades, use a hand sharpening stone to hone them off.

• A reel mower works on a scissors principle; the spiral blades on the reel shear off the grass by cutting against a fixed straight blade on the mower. If you look at this fixed blade you will notice that it can be adjusted. If it rubs too tightly against the reel, the mower will be hard to push; too loose and the grass isn't cut properly. In each case, mower life is shortened.

• Grass clippings quickly accumulate around the wheels and on other parts of the mower. These should be removed completely after each mowing. Otherwise, they will jam moving parts and encourage rusting.

• Avoid stones as much as possible. Use a mower on well-raked areas to prevent damage to the edges of the blades.

• Oil moving parts regularly and store off the ground between seasons.

Lawn sweepers.

• Take care of the sweeper the same as you would a reel-type mower. Keep clean and oiled.

• Pay particular attention to the brush that sweeps the debris into the canvas sling. It should be cleaned of any leaves and clippings after each use.

• If the canvas gets wet, let it dry in the sun if possible. The cloth will quickly deteriorate if it is stored wet or damp.

• When using the sweeper, empty it often. It is tempting to take another pass before dumping a load, but a heavy load puts a strain on the canvas and also makes the sweeper much harder to push.

The above list is not intended to cover every tool or piece of garden equipment you may own. However, we have given you the simple maintenance hints for a variety of implements. You will discover that it is easy to adapt these simple principles to anything you may own and increase the life of your tools many times over. Now let us take a look at your more expensive power-operated equipment.

Chapter 9

Small Gasoline Engines:

How to get the most from gas-powered equipment.

One of the greatest labor-saving innovations in years has been the use of the small gasoline-powered motor on a variety of home tools and equipment. A power mower, for example, is almost as much a part of a surburban home as the lawn. In addition, the gas motor is used on such helpers as snowblowers, chain saws, lawn vacuums, composters and shredders, and other outdoor conveniences.

The average owner who gives some care to a motor driven piece of equipment, seldom gets more than a third of the potential life built into today's small engines. Other owners who neglect simple maintenance details altogether often get only a tenth of what they should reasonably expect in service from an expensive tool or piece of equipment.

In this chapter we will tell you the simple things you can do to prolong the life of a gas engine at least two and maybe even as much as ten times. The things you need to do to achieve this bonus are neither difficult nor time consuming. You won't have to be a mechanic, either. This is *not* a chapter on motor repair or troubleshooting. Rather, the things we will show you are simple operations that will go a long way toward preventing expensive motor repairs, or the annoyance of balky operation.

TYPES OF GAS ENGINES

There are dozens of manufacturers of gas-powered equipment. However, most of them use engines manufactured by two or three of the major engine manufacturers. Because of this similarity in power plants, your job of preventive maintenance is considerably simplified. The motor on the lawn mower you use in the summer is probably the same as the motor on the snowblower you use in winter. Each is serviced identically.

The first thing you should be aware of is that motors are either two cycle or four cycle. You don't have to know how each operates in order to take care of them. However, there are very important things you must understand.

Two-cycle engines. If the nameplate indicates that it is a two-cycle engine, then it is vitally important that you observe the precise instructions for lubrication.

In a two-cycle engine, the lubricating oil is mixed with the gasoline and added to the gas tank. The gasoline evaporates and is burned in the engine to produce useful power. The oil separates out as a mist and lubricates the inside of the engine. Different engines require different proportions of gasoline and oil and these are shown on the engine. If the nameplate says to mix one-half pint of oil to each gallon of gasoline, follow that proportion exactly. Too much oil can be just as bad as too little. You can buy gas cans with measuring cups attached that are handy for mixing the oil and gasoline correctly.

Four-cycle engines. The nameplate that identifies the engine as a four-cycle engine will also tell you what grade of oil to use for lubrication. Ask your gas station attendant for the recommended grade and keep an extra can handy so you can add oil as needed during the season.

Refer to your owner's manual for exact instructions because methods of checking and filling the oil sump vary a little from model to model. Some engines have a simple dipstick that indicates oil level, while others have handy visible indicators that are somewhat less messy to use than a dipstick. Here are hints to make sure your engine doesn't wear out too quickly because of improper lubrication:

• Check your oil level *before* each use (Figure 9-1). If a dipstick is used, first pull it out and wipe it carefully with a rag. Then insert fully, remove carefully, and read the oil level. If the stick says to add oil, do it at once. Don't be tempted to give the lawn

Figure 9-1:   The first thing to do before using your mower is to check the oil level. Do this before each use.

another cutting because you don't have oil handy. That's why we suggested you always keep a spare can.

• On a new engine, change the oil after two hours of operation. During the break-in period, a new engine puts microscopic metal particles in the oil which can cause future damage. Draining the first oil filling will eliminate this potential for damage.

• Oil should be changed after every twenty-five hours of use. The job is easier if you do it immediately after using the equipment and the engine is still quite warm. Warm oil drains more quickly and thoroughly than cold oil. The oil-drain plug is usually at the lowest point on the machine and has a square head.

• Be careful about where you put the oil plug or the dipstick when changing or checking your oil. It's a good idea to wipe them off before replacing them in the motor. Any bit of dirt or grit that is picked up on these articles can find its way into the lubricating oil and do serious damage to the engine.

OTHER MAINTENANCE HINTS

Most small motors are designed to run at high speeds. This is much different than the engine in your car which works best at moderate speeds. At high speeds, it is easy to exceed safe limits and wear out parts quickly.

• The throttle or speed control on lawn mowers, blowers and other tools should be set so that the engine runs at about three-quarters of its maximum speed. Avoid the practice of running it at top speed at all times; this is like driving your car at 100 miles-an-hour all the time.

• If you overload the engine, it will labor and put excessive strain and pressure on important parts. Ease off on the load. If you're mowing a deep lawn, don't try to cut it in one pass. Rather, set the blade higher and mow in two lighter passes. This will save wear on the mower and time on your part.

• Make sure the idle and mixture controls are set according to the manufacturers recommendations. With proper maintenance, you shouldn't have to touch these adjustments for a long time.

• Lawn mowers and composters collect a lot of dirt and debris (Figure 9-2). Keep the engine clear of clippings and layers of oily dirt. These engines are air cooled and any accumulation of dirt on the fins of the engine will prevent heat from being dissipated, and the engine will run at dangerously high temperatures. (Figure 9-3.)

Fuel systems.

• Only fresh, clean gas should be put into the fuel tank. You may be surprised to learn that gasoline ages in a can and can gum up an engine if used later on. Therefore, don't store gasoline in a can over the winter and then try to use it in your mower when spring rolls around.

• The gas tank has a cap with a little hole in it. The hole lets air into the tank so the engine can suck gas into the carburetor. If this hole is clogged, the engine will be starved for gas and will run

Figure 9-2: **Automotive-type degreaser is handy for removing the oilsoaked dirt that accumulates on the deck.**

unpredictably. Keep this hole clean with a toothpick. If necessary, soak the cap in a solvent, like benzine, to keep this passage clean.

• Check your manual for the location of the fuel filter. Sometimes, you can see it readily on the outside. Often, however, the fuel filter is part of a tube that runs into the gas tank. The filter should be cleaned regularly, at least once each season.

Air systems.

• The air filter should be cleaned after 10 hours of use. If the engine is used in a very dusty location, this time should be shortened to every 4 or 6 hours.

• A paper or dry filter can be cleaned by removing it from the engine and rapping it on a hard surface to shake out dust particles. (Figure 9-4.) If it is very dirty, then simply replace it completely.

• Wet filters usually use a pad soaked in oil as a filter element. This pad should be cleaned in gasoline, squeezed dry, and

Figure 9-3:   **Use a strong stream from your hose to remove dirt and grease after treating with degreaser. Avoid squirting the water directly at the air intakes.**

then oiled with engine oil to renew its cleaning properties. Other wet filters use an oil bath through which the air passes. This should be cleaned by removing the dirty oil and caked-on dirt inside the filter cup, and then filling the cup with fresh oil up to a clearly-marked level.

   • Many small engines have small fans and shrouds to direct the flow of air around cooling fins. Make sure the shroud, fins or fan are not clogged with clippings or other debris that will cut down on the flow of air. An engine that operates at too high a temperature will wear out faster.

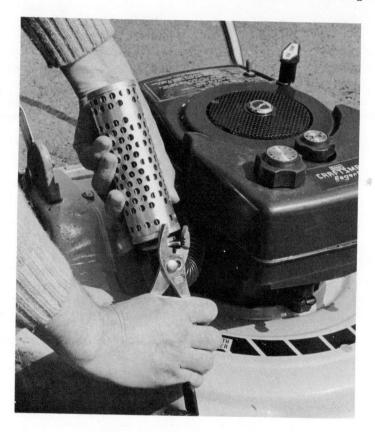

Figure 9-4:   A dry-type air cleaner is easily removed for cleaning with a pair of pliers.

Electrical systems.

• To work properly, the spark plug should be kept clean and properly gapped. The gap is the distance between the center and the ground electrodes on the tip of the plug. It is important that this distance be exactly what the manufacturer specifies in your owner's manual. You can buy an inexpensive tool that combines a thickness gage for measuring the gap, plus a small brush and file for cleaning the electrodes.

• Don't use a regular wrench to remove the plug. It is safer to use a special spark-plug wrench to prevent damage to the plug. Remove and check the plug after every 25 hours of use.

Figure 9-5: **Periodically, you should check all nuts and bolts on your equipment to make sure they are all tight.**

• The wire and clip that connect to the terminal on top of the plug should be kept bright and snug fitting. A loose wire can cause erratic running of the engine.

Mechanical systems.

• Keep linkages and springs free from dirt that could affect their operation. After cleaning, use light oil on pivots to keep all controls working smoothly.

• Once or twice each season you should check all the bolts and nuts for possible looseness (Figure 9-5). There is a lot of vibration associated with one cylinder engines that can cause them to come loose.

• If the piece of equipment is used on a seasonal basis, such as a mower or snowblower, you should take a few minutes to prepare the machine for storage between seasons. Drain the gas tank and run the engine to use up whatever gas is left in the carburetor. Afterwards, remove the spark plug and put about a tablespoon of

Figure 9-6:   **Before storing the motor for the season, remove the plug and squirt a tablespoon or so of engine oil into the cylinder. Work the motor by hand for a few revolutions to distribute the oil, and then replace the plug.**

heavy engine oil into the head of the engine. Turn the motor over by hand several times to distribute this oil. Replace the plug and store the machine in a warm, dry place. (Figure 9-6.)

TAKING CARE OF GAS-POWERED EQUIPMENT

Lawnmowers.

• Under no circumstances should you make any adjustments without first shutting off the machine. If you want to check the blade underneath, disconnect the spark plug wire to eliminate any possibility of the mower starting while you have your hands underneath the hood.

• The underside of the mower housing is designed aerodynamically. The air is sucked in from the underside, then lifts up the blades of grass for even cutting, and finally the clippings are blown out of the exhaust chute into a grass catcher. It is important that nothing interfere with this smooth flow of air under the housing. After each use, clean the housing of accumulated grass clippings with a wooden stick. A paint stirrer is ideal. If you wish, you can also wash away the debris with a hose set at full force (Figure 9-7). Afterwards, start the mower up and let it run a bit to dry out the underside to prevent corrosion.

Figure 9-7: **The underside of the deck of a mower will accumulate grass debris which cuts down on the suction action vital for even cutting. An easy way to remove such debris is with a hose.**

• On self-propelled mowers, clean the wheels thoroughly. If they accumulate grass clippings, they will spin and ruin your grass.

• Oil the wheel bearings regularly to make them last longer and to make your job of pushing the mower easier. (Figure 9-8.)

Figure 9-8: Keep all bearings running smoothly with regular lubrication.

• Empty the grass catcher frequently during use. If you let it get too full, not only do you overload the machine, but you will find that most of the clippings are not being picked up.

• Keep the blade sharp and balanced at all times. You can sharpen the blade with a grinder or file depending on how badly it is nicked. In either case, balance the blade on a nail through the center hole. If the blade isn't exactly level, take some metal off the heavy side. An out-of-balance blade can shake your mower apart and tire you out quickly.

Snowblowers.

• Know where you're pushing the revolving blades. On a smooth asphalt driveway you have no problem. However, be careful about cutting a swath over a stone driveway or similar location where the blade can pick up stones and hurl them around inside the blower housing.

• After each use, brush away all the snow from the blades and from inside the housing. This is to minimize melting and the attendant problems of corrosion.

• Lubricate the machine according to specifications. Cold weather is hard on joints and bearings because cold oil does not lubricate efficiently.

Cultivators.

• In hard, clay soil, you will put less strain on the machine and yourself if you cultivate to the desired depth by making more than one pass with the machine. This is especially important if you have large stones in the ground.

• Most tillers have a worm-gear drive to revolve the tines. It is important that the worm housing be kept properly greased.

• After each use, remove mud and dirt from the tines and the underside of the tiller. Wet mud will harden in joints and cause excessive wear.

• Edges and trimmers should be handled the same way.

Composters.

• Don't exceed the capacity of the machine indicated in the instructions. Branches larger than recommended can jam the inside and damage the chipping mechanism.

• Some machines have a safety door that springs open to release a large object, like a rock, that can't be ground in the mill. Make sure the spring door mechanism is working properly before you start the mill. A struck door can cause the rock or stone to break the chipping blades.

Outboard motors.

• After a season of wear, water and storage, the first thing you should check before going out on the water is the starter rope. If the rope is frayed or worn, replace it at once. You can sit for a long time on the water if your starter rope is broken.

• Check filters, hoses and spark plugs as previously suggested. However, because safety is involved, replace worn parts if you have the slightest doubt about their ability to stand up to another season of wear.

• Lubricate the grease fittings on the swivel pins to keep them working smoothly and to prevent wear.

• Check the propeller for fishing line wound around the shaft. This can cause all sorts of problems if neglected.

• Check the propeller for nicks or broken pieces. Small nicks can be filed out. If a larger section of the blade is missing, then replace the propeller because it will be out of balance, and produce undue wear and vibration.

The modern gas-powered engine is a long-lasting efficient power source for a variety of household chores. The simple steps we've outlined above should enable you to get several times the useful life you may have thought possible. We end with one final word of caution: Gas-powered equipment produces the same deadly carbon monoxide as does your automobile engine. *Never* run such equipment in a closed space, such as a garage.

Chapter 10

Garden Furniture:

How to increase the life of your outdoor furniture.

Here are some suggestions to keep in mind as you look at furniture made of different materials. Each material has some advantages and disadvantages. It's up to you to decide which one you think will be easier to care for in the particular situation you have in mind.

Iron and steel. These metals rust quickly unless protected from moisture. Wrought iron has to be painted regularly. To prevent rust from getting a foothold, you have to be prepared for frequent touch-ups in the course of a season as paint wears or chips off.

Steel is usually found in the form of springs supporting various padding materials. In this form it can't be painted and the only practical maintenance is to bring the furniture into a protected shelter every night.

With these metals you have to decide whether the appearance of the piece you want is worth the time and trouble of maintaining it. With proper care, such furniture will wear a long time and outlast anything made of wood, aluminum, or other non-rusting materials.

Aluminum. This is a popular material for lightweight lawn furniture because it doesn't rust in the usual sense. Aluminum oxidizes in weathering and turns a dull color. This oxide film can be removed, if you wish, with some fine steel wool much as you would polish an aluminum pot in your kitchen.

If you want to know what you're paying for, check the thickness of the metal before you buy a piece. An easy way to do this with a chair, for example, is to pull off the tip on the bottom of the leg and look at the thickness of the tubing. Compare two lawn chairs of different prices and you'll see a difference in tubing.

Wood. Redwood is traditionally the choice of outdoor furniture because of its attractive color and durability. For very rustic furniture, other woods are used, particularly cedar. Don't be misled into thinking that such furniture can be left outdoors without any worry about maintenance.

Redwood will remain attractive in color only if it is protected with a coat of special redwood stain and sealer, or ordinary linseed oil. This coating has to be renewed at least every season if you want the pieces to remain good looking (Figure 10-1.) Without this seal coat, redwood quickly weathers to an undistinguished grey color, although its strength and durability are unaffected. Some builders will substitute fir for redwood in building an outdoor deck or porch, and stain it to look like redwood. Regular use of outdoor wood preservative is necessary on the less durable woods if you want long life. Ideally, all joints should be constructed with rust-resistant bolts. Bolts can be tightened as the wood shrinks, something you can't do with nails.

Other woods, such as pine, are usually painted and require normal repainting at frequent intervals to maintain appearance and to prevent the wood from weathering.

Plastics. A variety of plastics are used in outdoor furniture, and can often be the most worry free. As with aluminum, you will discover a wide difference in prices based on the thickness of the plastic.

Upholstery materials. All types are used. Before buying, ask specifically what is inside the padding, or look at the tag that is required on every upholstered piece. Regardless of how weatherproof the covering is, minute holes around the stitching will allow moisture to penetrate inside the padding. Even with urethane foams and similar materials, there is some risk of moisture causing mildew or rot; with organic fibers such as sisal, you risk faster deterioration and discomfort.

Figure 10-1: **Redwood furniture needs an annual coating of sealer and stain to keep it good looking and to make it last longer.**

STORAGE OF OUTDOOR FURNITURE

Ideally, it would be wonderful if you could simply store your furniture outdoors where you use it. A lot of people do just this, particularly with aluminum furniture. To insure longer life, you should make some arrangement for storing the pieces, especially to protect them from winter ravages.

Smaller pieces, such as chairs can be hung up in a garage (Figure 10-2). Other items can be disassembled and brought into basements, breezeways, or other sheltered places. The important thing to remember is that the life of every piece will be significantly shortened if you simply leave it out in the open four seasons a year.

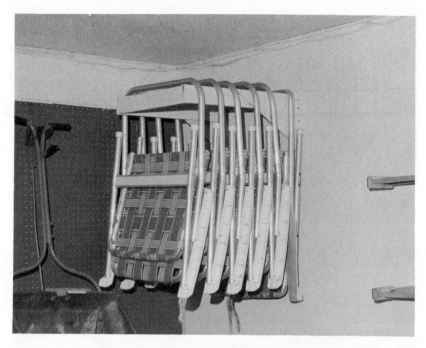

Figure 10-2: A simple wooden rack near the garage ceiling is a great place to store garden furniture and to prevent damage. It's a good idea to hang up everything possible to make for efficiency.

MAINTENANCE OF OUTDOOR FURNITURE

Here are specific techniques for maintaining good looks and increasing the useful life of the more common outdoor articles you own:

Wrought iron. With care, you can have good looking wrought iron furniture that will last practically forever.

• Before painting, wirebrush thoroughly and prime rust spots with special rust-inhibiting primer.

• Use special rust-preventive paints that are available for outdoor furniture.

• Be alert to rust spots, particularly at joints or where the paint may have chipped off. Touch up at once to prevent the spread of rust stains. A spray can of paint is handy for this.

• If you have a number of paint coats that chip off in thick flakes, consider removing the paint down to the bare metal. On wrought iron you can do this with paint remover.

Steel. Steel is used in flat springs, coil springs, and for hardware such as bolts and screws. Most of the time, preventing rust is a matter of preventing moisture from getting to the parts.

• Parts with steel springs should not be left out to weather.

• Steel bolts and rivets are often used because of strength requirements. These should be protected with a coat of paint or clear lacquer. If the part moves, for example the hinge pin in a lawn chair, protect it with a thin film of white grease available in a sewing-machine store.

Aluminum. Even though aluminum doesn't rust, you can prolong its life with simple maintenance techniques.

• Dulling oxide films can be removed with fine steel wool and soap. Here and there you may discover more serious pitting or tougher stains. In such cases, try fine scouring powder. Aluminum is sensitive to certain chemicals, particularly strong alkalis, so be sure to rinse immediately and thoroughly with plenty of clean water.

• Remember that aluminum is rather soft. Avoid any use that will increase the wear unduly. For example, on a rough concrete patio see if you can protect the wearing surfaces of the aluminum furniture with other materials. Dragging soft aluminum on concrete is almost like putting a piece of metal up against a grindstone.

• Check mechanical joints frequently for looseness. Self-tapping steel screws are often used on aluminum to hold parts together. If the screw loosens even slightly, it will enlarge the hole to the point where it will be impossible to tighten the screw to hold properly.

Wood. Wood is versatile and good looking. As a general rule, however, it requires more care than aluminum or plastic to maintain long life.

• Redwood furniture requires a once-a-year job of sealing and staining to maintain looks and life. Before using any of the many products available for this purpose, make sure the surface is clean of any grease. A summer of drippy hamburgers and barbequed chicken can leave a lot of grease behind.

• If possible, store wood furniture indoors during the winter. If you have no room, try upending the furniture against the most protected side of your house. The idea is to prevent large areas of wood from being covered with snow and then being subjected to alternate thawing and freezing of water.

• The first place to rot or wear is the part of the leg that rests on the ground. Here's a good maintenance technique for handling such trouble spots:

Put each leg in a large coffee can and pour some wood preservative in each can. Let the legs soak like this for twenty-four hours or longer, adding more preservative as it is absorbed.

• Tighten all hardware at least once a season. Loose bolts and screws not only make the furniture feel wobbly, but tremendously increase the wear on holes and joints.

• Benches and other articles made of pine should be painted with an outdoor enamel.

• On furniture with spindles, make sure the joints are always tight. You can tighten such joints several ways. Drill a small hole in the joint, fill with glue, and then force a wooden matchstick down as far as possible. If you can get a disposable hypodermic syringe from your doctor, fill it with liquid wood glue, and then inject each joint as deeply as possible.

Plastics. Plastics for outdoor use come in many forms. Thick and rigid forms are used for weight-bearing members; rope and webbing is used on aluminum chairs; and plastic fabrics are used to cover and upholster a variety of things.

• Remember that even the best plastics are soft and never as strong as aluminum or wood. Avoid dragging plastic articles in a way that will cause undue stress or wear.

• Certain plastics are affected by pool chemicals—ask which before you buy.

• Most plastics should be cleaned with mild soap and water. Avoid harsh chemicals, particularly those containing abrasives.

• Plastic webbing will last longer if all the strips in a piece of furniture are kept tight. Once a single strip gets loose, the other strips are put under excess strain and quickly rip.

• Webbing is usually kept in place with steel screws that have fairly large heads to grip the plastic. Check these points often, because most wear begins here. It's an easy matter to loosen the screw, pull the webbing tight, and use a new spot on the webbing for passing through the screw. (Figure 10-3.)

Figure 10-3: **It is an easy matter to remove worn webbing from aluminum furniture, and replace it with fresh webbing, available in long rolls. This will automatically double the life of such furniture.**

Upholstery.

• If pads get wet, wipe off with a dry cloth and hang to dry so both sides get air and light. This should be done whether the padding is weatherproof or not.

• Make a spot especially handy for storing such pads. Then, when night falls or rain threatens, you can quickly put away such articles with a minimum of fuss. Make this a habit.

• Remember that coverings on pads are especially vulnerable to damage and stains when used outdoors. Plastic coverings are easily ripped with sharp articles, such as shoe buckles. Grass stains and suntan oils are impossible to remove completely from canvas or cotton coverings.

• In general, use pads on the furniture for which they were designed. Avoid taking a pad off a chaise, for example, and using it on the ground where it will wear and get dirty quickly.

Barbeque grills.

• Hot charcoal will quickly ruin the bottom of the sheet-metal firebox in the grills. Prevent the charcoal from actually touching the steel bottom in any of several ways. Put a layer of clean sand on the bottom at least an inch thick and build your charcoal fire on top of that. Or, place a layer of heavy foil on the bottom and put the charcoal on that. A handy item is a disposable broiler tray which you can throw away later with the ashes.

• After cooling, clean out the ashes. Have an old broom remnant or brush handy, and clean away ashes that have accumulated on other parts of the grill.

• The food-holding grids should be cleaned with hot water and strong detergents. You can make the cleaning job easier if you remove the grids and lay them aside as soon as you're finished cooking. Don't let the food bake on while you eat!

• Many grills have mechanisms for raising or lowering the grid or the firebox. To keep these working smoothly, keep them free from rust by frequent cleaning with coarse steel wool. Lubrication is tough in a high-heat situation, but you can try wiping moving joints with a cloth lightly moistened with plain mineral oil. Don't use motor oil or similar lubricants if there is any possibility that it will get on to the food being prepared.

• Clean up grease splatters promptly with a good detergent and water. Then dry off all the parts carefully to prevent rust.

• Touch up rust spots with special rust-inhibiting paint before they get too serious. Sheet metal is relatively thin and a rust spot can quickly go right through the metal leaving nothing but a hole.

• A grill should be brought in at night, especially if there is a possibility of rain. If you can't bring the grill in, then protect it with a cover. An inexpensive one can be improvised from a large plastic trash can liner.

Umbrellas.

• A large picnic-table umbrella has a hanging ring on the end. This means you should take down the umbrella after each use and hang it up. This is the best way of storing an umbrella to prevent anything from bending the ribs.

• If you put a large hook in a protected spot outside, you'll be more inclined to take down the umbrella and store it properly at night. A corner, under a soffit or roof overhang if it is low enough, is the ideal spot for storing your umbrella.

• Never leave your umbrella open all night or during a windy session. Even a light wind puts strains on an umbrella when it is fully open. If the umbrella is connected to a table, a gust of wind can ruin both umbrella and table.

• Wash your umbrella cover frequently with a detergent and a long-handled brush. A brush that can be connected to a garden hose, ordinarily used for washing cars, is ideal for this job.

• After the fabric goes on the umbrella, you still should have a perfectly usable frame if you've taken care of the aluminum pole and ribs. Usually, you can get a new umbrella cover for a fraction of the cost of a new umbrella, and you can install it easily yourself. The only tool you need is a pair of pliers.

• When storing the umbrella between seasons, a trash can liner makes an ideal cover for protecting it from dirt and weather, even if it is stored outdoors. Just cut a tiny slit, to let the top ring pass through, so you can hang the umbrella up.

Folding chairs and other furniture.

• Avoid oil on joints unless it is unlikely that clothing will come in contact with the joint. Rather, use the white grease usually sold for sewing-machine motors and similar equipment. After working it into the joint, wipe off all excess.

• Wheels should get careful oiling to prevent rust on the axles. If the wheels are wood, try rubbing paraffin inside the hole to keep the wheel from absorbing moisture and rusting the axle.

• Fold and unfold such furniture frequently during the season, especially if you've worked oil or grease into the joints. This will help work the lubricant down where it is needed, keeping the article easy to use.

Miscellaneous outdoor furniture and appliances. By now, even if an item you own hasn't been mentioned, you should have a good idea what to do to make it last a lot longer than you may have originally expected or hoped.

Some passing hints:

• Be alert to anything that can collect water. Tables with rims are a good example. If you can't take them in at night, at least tip them over on their sides so a sudden rain doesn't create a puddle on the top.

• The bottoms of furniture take a terrible beating outside. Aluminum furniture should have easily-renewable plastic tips. Wooden table legs should get a preservative treatment once a year. If possible, outdoor furniture should be lifted from place to place and not dragged.

• Keep a supply of repair parts or materials on hand. To delay a repair usually means that it gets worse very fast. It is an easy matter to replace a broken piece of webbing on a chair as soon as the break occurs. But to let it go usually means a big repair job—someone will sit on the chair and the remaining webs will part very quickly.

• Finishing materials should be chosen for outdoor durability. Shellac, for example, is not waterproof and should not be used on outdoor furniture. Rather, you should choose such things as spar varnish, outdoor stains and sealers, and outdoor-trim enamels for painted pieces.

• Finally, remember that old-fashioned paste wax—the kind that used to be used on automobiles in the old days? It is a remarkably good preservative on all kinds of outdoor articles, particularly wood and painted metal surfaces. Not only will a coat of wax extend the life of the finish, and therefore the piece the finish is protecting, but it is a lot easier to apply the wax than to refinish the whole piece.

While no one wants to become a slave to the things he or she may own, maintenance of outdoor furniture is not really a difficult or time-consuming task. The preceding pointers should convince you that getting twice the life and enjoyment out of the things you own and use outdoors is easy if you tackle the jobs while they are still small.

Chapter 11

Sports, Hobby and Recreational Equipment:

How to make your leisure time more enjoyable.

Sports and hobby equipment is bought with one purpose in mind: to give pleasure and enjoyment during leisure-time activities. Often, however, this goal is frustrated because the user is unfamiliar with the special precautions needed to make this expensive equipment give additional years of service.

Many types of sports equipment are used only during certain seasons. Long months of neglect, or improper storage, can shorten the useful life appreciably, cause unnecessary disappointment, and expensive replacement. While we can't cover every type of leisure activity in these pages, we will give you the highlights of good care for the most popular types of sports and hobbies.

ARCHERY

• Proper stringing is the most important step in prolonging bow life and in shooting accurately. Put equal pressure on each bow limb when stringing as follows: Stand with your legs about two feet apart. One bow limb should rest on your left foot; the middle of the bow should be braced against the back of your right knee (in other words, the bow is between your legs); and the other bow limb should come up near your right arm. By leaning forward, you will automatically put equal stress on each limb, and prevent damage.

192

• Make sure the string grooves in the bow are clean. It's a good idea to carry a toothbrush with you in the field so you can clean them as needed. Dirt in the string groove will cause the bow limb to twist, make for inaccurate shooting, and shorten string life.

• Keep the bow clean with a silicone "gun cloth" available in sporting shops. Scratches can be eliminated with ordinary furniture polish when you get home.

• Protect the bow from extreme changes in humidity, and put it away unstrung.

• Every time you string your bow is a good time to check the string. String life can be prolonged by using special string wax or ordinary beeswax.

• Arrows will last a long time if you observe this most important rule: When removing the arrow from either target or game, grasp the arrow as close as possible to the imbedded point and pull straight out. Grabbing the arrow in the middle and trying to twist it out will damage the arrow.

• Hunting arrows, or broadheads, should be kept as sharp as possible. Therefore, when carrying them in the field, don't let them rattle around in a quiver with the edges rubbing against each other. Use a special holder to keep the heads from hitting each other.

BASEBALL EQUIPMENT

• A baseball glove should be kept dry. Leaving it in a damp place will quickly ruin the leather and make it impossible to form a good pocket for the ball.

• Neatsfoot oil should be used regularly on the glove to preserve it and keep it supple.

• Worn lacings should be replaced before they break completely. Glove life will be shortened if you play with broken lacings.

• Baseballs are expendable. However, you can keep playing longer if you keep them dry. Don't let baseballs lie on a damp lawn overnight.

• Wiping off the dirt with a damp rag after play will keep the balls looking new longer, and also prevent dried grit from working into the stitching and shortening the playing life.

• Bats should also be wiped free of dirt and moisture after use.

• For storage, hang bats by the end in any sort of homemade bat holder.

BICYCLES

• Make sure the seat, handlebars, and pedal distance are all properly adjusted for your height. If you don't "fit" your bike, chances are you will strain it unnecessarily and shorten its life.

• The bicycle chain should be kept free from dirt and lubricated with special chain lubricant. First spray the chain with bicycle degreaser, wipe clean, and then lubricate with chain lubricant. Use a toothbrush and a soft cloth to clean the chain thoroughly (Figure 11-1).

Figure 11-1: **A toothbrush and soft rag will keep the chain on your bike clean and working smoothly.**

• Wipe accumulated dirt and grime from gears and derailleurs as often as required. Put oil very sparingly on pivots, to avoid attracting more dirt. Keeping this mechanism clean will repay you with smooth, trouble-free shifting for a long time.

• Lightly oil the pivot bolt of caliper brakes. At the same time, make sure the wheel rims are free of dirt, oil, or wax so that the brakes can work efficiently. Never wax the rims.

• Brake and derailleur cables should be removed from their housings and greased periodically so that they work smoothly. Brakes and gears will require adjustment after this operation so you may want to leave this job for a bike shop to do once a year.

• Front and rear sprockets should be cleaned at the same time, in the same way you clean the chain.

• Regularly inspect your bike for any loose bolts or nuts and tighten as necessary.

• Wheel and crank bearings should be disassembled, cleaned and lubricated periodically. Again, you might want to leave this job for the bike shop with its special know-how and tools.

• Get some touch-up paint and keep it handy for covering scratches and nicks in the finish. Apart from preserving a new look, such care will prevent rust from starting.

• To prevent premature wear, your tires should be inflated to the proper pressure. This varies with the size of the tire and is usually marked on the tire. If not, consult your owner's manual.

• Slight misalignments in wheels or fenders can cause undue wear on tires. Make sure tires run smoothly without any rubbing anywhere (Figure 11-2).

• Follow the maker's instructions on proper methods of shifting gears if your bicycle is so equipped. In general: You should shift only when wheels and pedals are moving; never try to shift while pedals are moving backwards; shift one or two gears at a time; and ease up somewhat on pedal pressure when you're shifting.

• Finally, the best way to insure long years of enjoyment from your bike is to invest in a strong bicycle lock, and *use* it. Like a car, a bike is both loot and a getaway vehicle to a thief. Be careful whenever you leave your bike. Record the serial number for possible recovery and identification later on.

BILLIARDS

• Make sure the pool table is level and firmly supported on all legs. Slight misalignments can cause undue stresses in the table and affect the accuracy of the game.

**Figure 11-2:   Check the wheels frequently to make sure they run true
and do not rub against the fender, frame, or brake pads.**

• Use a brush on the cloth before play to remove dust and
dirt, and to freshen the nap of the cloth. A hand vacuum is also
handy (Figure 11-3).

• Caution beginning players on proper play. Often a beginner
will be carried away by the excitement of the game and try fancy
jump shots that can rip the cloth.

• Pool cues should·be stored in a cue rack to keep them
straight. Leaning them against walls is the quickest way to ruin
them.

• Billiard balls are precision things. Treat them as such to
preserve long, accurate playing life. In other words, don't let them
drop on the floor through carelessness or wild shooting.

Figure 11-3:   **A small vacuum cleaner is ideal to keep a billiard cloth in top shape.**

BINOCULARS AND TELESCOPES

• Always carry binoculars or telescopes in cases, removing them only when you want to use them.

• If lens caps are provided, replace them whenever you put away the glasses.

• Never touch the lenses with anything except the softest tissue or special lens paper. If you avoid putting fingerprints on the lenses, it is surprising how long they will go before they need to be cleaned.

• Brush or blow off grit and dust before cleaning the lenses (Figure 11-4). Then breathe lightly on the lens and wipe with a soft tissue. Do not use silicone treated lens paper on coated lenses. Such lens paper is designed only for spectacles.

• Avoid getting dirt into the focusing mechanisms; grit will quickly affect the smoothness of operation that is vital for easy use.

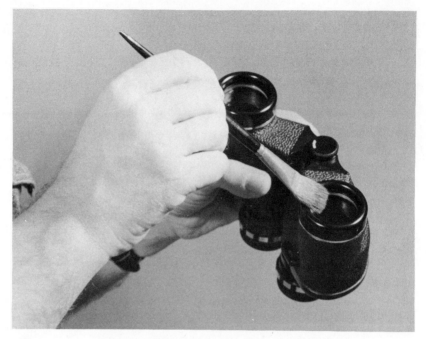

Figure 11-4:   **Before cleaning lenses on binoculars or cameras with soft tissue, brush away any dust or grit with a soft brush.**

BOATS AND CANOES

• The best time for boat maintenance is in the Fall after the boat is out of the water. If you wait till Spring, rust and rot can take their toll, and you'll probably do a hurry-up job because you are anxious to get the boat back in the water.

• Thorough cleaning, inside and out, is the first and most important step in preserving your boat for additional seasons. Scrub the bottom; clean topside; and vacuum in every corner and all the upholstery. Open all hatches and ventilate the inside as much as possible to prevent dry rot.

• Store boats out of the weather. If you don't have inside storage, make sure the boat is protected with a weatherproof cover.

• Small boats may be stored in your garage. Rig up some device to hold the boat or canoe up near the ceiling. This will keep it out of the way and also prevent the accidental punctures that are likely if the craft is stored on the floor.

• Rubber boats should be stored partially inflated away from heat or direct sunlight. It's also a good idea to dust talcum powder lightly on the surface.

• Painting and varnishing are regular chores for owners of wooden boats. The biggest mistake made by many boat owners is to skimp on surface preparation. Unless you are prepared to invest the time to do the job properly, and the money on proper tools (like a heavy-duty belt sander), you might better leave this job to a professional.

• Sails should be washed free of salt water and thoroughly dry before storage. The same is true of ropes.

• All gasoline should be drained from the tank, carburetor, and fuel lines, otherwise it will turn to varnish by the beginning of the next season, and you'll have an expensive job to undo the damage.

BOOTS

• Leather boots should be cleaned and waterproofed several times a season. Scrape off thick dirt or mud with a dull knife; use saddle soap liberally, using a toothbrush to get into seams and crevices; finish with a commercial silicone waterproof sealer.

• If your boots get wet, turn them upside down and let them dry away from too much heat. Stuffing newspaper down in the toes will only impede air circulation and prolong drying time.

• Between seasons, store boots in a warm, dry place. Damp locations, like a corner of a basement, will probably cause mildew to form.

• Rubber boots and waders should be stored upside down on some sort of rack. In particular, avoid folding long tops over for periods of time. Otherwise, you'll find a permanent crease that will cause the rubber to come apart.

• Sprinkling the insides of boots with talcum powder will prolong the life of the rubber and make the boots easier to put on.

CAMERAS

• Store and carry your camera properly. Keep it in the case until you are ready to take pictures. Don't store the camera in places where it will be subjected to great variations in temperature or humidity; in particular, never leave the camera in a hot, automobile glove compartment.

• Moisture is a great enemy of your camera, so be careful about taking pictures in the rain, in boats or at the seashore. If your camera falls overboard, wipe thoroughly and get it to a repair shop as soon as possible.

• Know how to operate all the controls before you use the camera. If anything appears stiff or hard to turn, *don't force!* Get someone who knows to help you.

• The lens is an incredibly complicated arrangement of precision glass and metal components. Handle the lens carefully at all times, and be especially careful about the delicate glass surface. Never touch it with your fingers or anything other than a lens brush or lens cleaning tissue.

• If the lens appears dirty, the first thing to do is to blow or brush away any particles of dust or grit, however small. A gritty particle left on the lens will scratch the surface when you try cleaning it with lens tissue. After this step, put a drop of special lens cleaning solution on the surface and gently wipe the whole surface with special lens tissue. Both these articles are available at every camera shop and should be as much a part of your camera case as a roll of film.

• If your camera takes interchangeable lenses, be very careful when changing and storing the different lenses. Even though it takes a few moments more, it is a good idea to put caps on both ends of the lens before putting it in its own case for additional protection. (Figure 11-5.)

• Read your instruction booklet carefully and follow any special maintenance steps recommended by the manufacturer. With some cameras, this means replacing batteries at regular intervals, wiping rollers, cleaning the interior, or other vital steps necessary to keep the camera working properly and producing the kind of pictures you want.

CAMPING GEAR

• Transport non-electric lanterns in a vertical position to protect glass globes and to prevent fuel from leaking out.

• Keep lanterns clean, being especially careful to wipe up any spills of liquid fuel.

Figure 11-5: **Changing lenses on cameras which accept interchangeable lenses can be less dangerous if you first put on the lens cap to protect the delicate surface from fingerprints or scratches. All adjustments on cameras should be handled gently; don't force!**

• Valves, pump plungers, and other moving parts on your lantern should always be tightened "finger-tight". Do not use excessive force or you may wind up stripping threads. (Figure 11-6.)

• The pump on some lanterns is similar to a bicycle pump that uses a leather washer as a piston. Check this washer every couple of months and if it appears dry, soak it in light oil for a couple of hours.

• Camp stoves collect a lot of grease from cooking which can quickly clog orifices. Wipe up grease spills quickly.

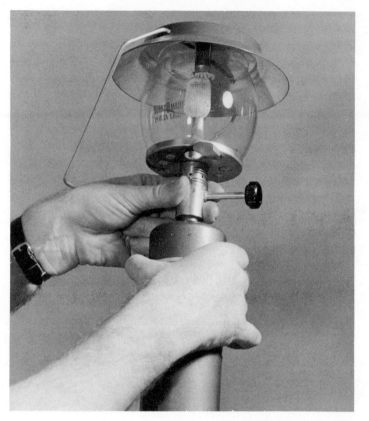

Figure 11-6:   **Adjustments on propane equipment should be done only with fingers. Never force with pliers or wrenches.**

• Catalytic heaters should be stored without fuel between uses, and stored upright at all times to prevent the fuel from leaking and causing damage.

• Cooling equipment such as jugs, Thermos bottles, ice chests and the like quickly collect odors which may discourage you from using them. Baking soda and fresh air will keep such items sweet smelling for a long time.

• If your ice chest or cooler has a rubber gasket around the lid, you can preserve its flexibility and sealing qualities by dusting it with talcum powder each time you wash it.

• A wooden backpacking frame should be varnished with spar varnish to make it last longer.

• Canvas packs should be thoroughly cleaned after each camping trip. If you leave particles of food in the pack, you may attract destructive vermin.

• Aluminum wear gets rather black and sooty in camp. Don't bother trying to clean outsides of pots and pans while in camp. When you get home, use trisodium phosphate and hot water (wear rubber gloves) to do a quick job of cleaning.

CHAIN SAWS

• The most important rule is to keep your chain sharp and well oiled. Use the oiler built into the saw according to your instructions.

• Never put away a saw with a dirty chain, especially if it is clogged with moisture-laden sawdust. It doesn't hurt to remove the chain and put it to soak in a pan of oil until you're ready to use the saw again.

• Chain tension should be checked before each use. A loose chain is a dangerous thing, while a chain that is too tight will wear quickly and overload the motor.

• Oiled-soaked sawdust will quickly collect on the motor and clog filters and moving parts. Keep the saw clean. Further hints on taking care of a small gasoline motor are found in Chapter 9.

FISHING GEAR

• Try to keep your tackle box closed between uses. Leaving it open, especially if you're in a boat and it is raining, will mess up all the things carried by a fisherman in his box.

• A worn rod can be refurbished for far less than the cost of a new one. Broken handles can be replaced with new cork, new ferrules and guides can be installed at little cost, and the whole rod refinished with special rod varnish to give many more years of use.

• Reels must be cleaned and lubricated according to instructions. In fact, it isn't a bad idea to strip down a new reel even before you use it. This way, you'll know what to do when you're out on the water and some adjustment is needed.

• Don't put away a dirty reel at the end of a season. If you do, you won't have one for the beginning of the new season.

• Nets should be thoroughly dried before folding and storing.

GOLFING EQUIPMENT

No real golfer would neglect the things that bring such joy to his life. However, even the fussiest golfer may find these hints useful.

• Oil and perspiration on grips can be removed easily with alcohol (Figure 11-7).

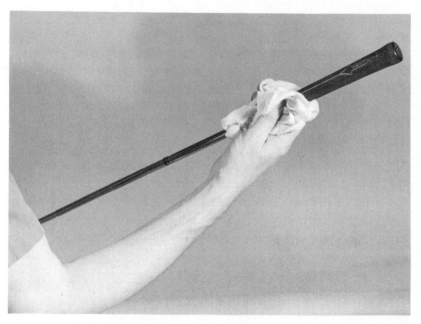

Figure 11-7: **Golf clubs are easily cleaned of perspiration and body oils with a rag moistened in alcohol. Cover knicks on wooden parts with dark shoe polish.**

• Clean the shafts with an alcohol moistened rag. Now and then, rub shoe polish on the heads of woods to hide nicks and scratches and to give a shine.

• A fine wire-brush wheel that will fit your power drill or drill press is a great way to keep the heads of metal clubs free from rust.

• Don't neglect your golf cart. The wheels pick up a lot of mud and dirt when rolled over damp or wet grounds. Keep the wheels clean and the axles oiled to prevent rust and ensure free wheeling.

GUNS

• Moisture, whether it comes from condensation, your fingertips, or from the sky as rain, is the agent that will do the most damage to a gun. Therefore, after each use or handling, make sure you wipe away all traces of moisture.

• Cleaning the gun is vitally important if you want it to last a long time. If you don't know how to clean a gun, you shouldn't own one. However, even experienced gun owners will often overoil a gun after cleaning.

• After oiling separate parts, let them drain on a clean cloth before re-assembling. This allows excess oil to drain away. Also, when storing a gun after cleaning, it should go muzzle down to let oil drain out of the barrel.

• Never store a gun in a cloth or leather carrying case. Such cases absorb moisture and will rust the gun quickly.

• Blueing on a gun serves two purposes: it prevents rust, and also improves the appearance of the gun. If the blueing on your gun is worn, consider using one of the cold blueing kits available at gun shops.

• Keep the finish on the stock in good repair to prevent deterioration of the wood. A good penetrating finish is old-fashioned boiled linseed oil, well rubbed in.

HOME ENTERTAINMENT EQUIPMENT

• Stay out of the insides of your TV. Voltages up to 25,000 volts are stored there, even after the set is unplugged from the wall outlet. Leave all that tinkering to a pro and both you and your TV will last longer.

• Dirty antenna leads, particularly on an outside antenna can cause a weak or ghostly picture. Check these leads and make sure the antenna is pointed toward the stations you want to receive. As you rotate the antenna slightly, have someone watch the set and yell when the picture appears best. Mark this position and check every few months, especially if you are subject to high winds.

• Instant-on sets are really on all the time, although at a reduced level of current consumption. If you're going to be away for a time, it is wise to unplug the set from the wall.

• On portable radios, remove the batteries if you are not going to use the set for several weeks. This is to prevent damage to the set from batteries that are defective and which may leak.

• Amplifiers, tuners, and receivers can use either tubes or solid-state components. Tube equipment generates considerable heat so that the set should be located in a ventilated area if you want long life from the equipment. Solid-state equipment is less needful of good ventilation.

• Twice a year you should disconnect the components and use the brush attachment on your vacuum cleaner to pick up accumulated dust.

• If you want to do minor repairs which involve soldering, remember that solid-state equipment is very delicate and easily damaged by heat. Don't use a soldering gun on such equipment. Rather, use a small pencil-type soldering iron of about 25 watts.

• A record player should be kept clean and free from dust. Check your owner's manual to see if any periodic lubrication is necessary.

• Don't plug the record player into a convenience outlet on some other component. Instead, plug the record player into its own outlet in the wall. The reason for this precaution is to prevent damage to the idler wheel inside the record player. If plugged into a convenience outlet, you might turn off the component, and the record player, while the player is still in part of the cycle where the idler is pressing against a drive wheel. Prolonged pressure of the idler will cause a low spot to develop, and affect the speed of the turntable.

• Speakers should not be overloaded with too powerful amplifiers. Make sure the speaker is matched to the amplifier to prevent tearing of the paper cone or burning of the coil.

• For the best sound, keep recording heads on tape recorders absolutely clean. Use a cotton swab moistened with alcohol to clean the metal. This step will also prolong tape life.

• Records should not be stored in places where they are subject to high heat or humidity. Keep them in their protective jackets until you are ready to play them. In particular, avoid any situation which would cause the records to warp, such as putting them down on an irregular surface.

ICE SKATES

- Use saddle soap and neatsfoot oil to keep the leather shoe part of the skate in top shape.
- After use, wipe off all moisture to prevent rust to runners.
- Protect sharp runners with rubber or plastic protectors available in sporting stores. The less you need to sharpen, the longer the skates will last.
- Treat roller skates the same way, except that the rollers should be lubricated with a graphite compound. Oil can gum, and reduce your speed.

LUGGAGE

- Don't store plastic luggage where it can be damaged by sharp articles. Some plastics get a permanent "set" quite easily, so be careful of folding or denting the surface by improper storage.
- Leather luggage should be cared for the same way as other leather goods. Clean soil off with a sudsy mixture of warm water and saddle soap. Then protect the leather with a good rubbing of neatsfoot oil.
- Fabric luggage should be cleaned with mild suds and warm water, using a small brush in a circular motion. Wipe off with a damp cloth. Proper cleaning not only keeps the luggage looking new longer, but also helps you spot small rips and tears which can be repaired before they become serious.
- Locks and hardware should be kept working smoothly with a touch of graphite lubricant on moving parts and joints.

SKIS

- Skis should always be stored upright between seasons. In particular, never lay them on the ground where something can rest on them and destroy the camber built into the skis.
- Put a block of foam plastic in the middle of the skis, and then tie top and bottom together with straps. This will preserve the camber during storage. (Figure 11-8.)
- Hang up poles when not in use. This will prevent someone from stepping on them and bending them. The baskets should not

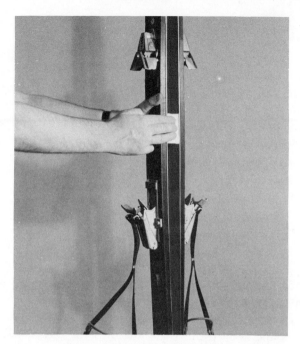

Figure 11-8:   **Camber can be preserved in skis between seasons if you put a soft block of styrofoam in the center, and then fasten tops and bottoms together with elastic ski straps.**

touch anything, otherwise they will assume a bend relative to the handle.

• Boots, if leather, should be treated like other leather articles with saddle soap and neatsfoot oil. Plastic boots should be cleaned with warm, soapy water. A boot caddy is a good investment to keep your boots in good shape longer, both while storing and transporting them to the ski area.

SLEEPING BAGS

• Sleeping bags will get wet on a camping trip no matter how hard you try to avoid it. Try to dry them as quickly as possible.

• Before storing, unroll and unzip completely. Then brush out all dirt that could attract vermin, making sure the bag is completely dry before you start to roll it up for storage.

• The zipper can be made to last a long time and work with silky smoothness if you rub a candle up and down the teeth every so often. The paraffin in the candle is a perfect zipper lubricant.

• Clean the bag according to the manufacturer's instructions at regular intervals. Again, this is a great opportunity to take care of minor repairs so they will not become major on a camping trip.

TENNIS EQUIPMENT

• Always keep your racket dry. Never store it in a high-humidity location, regardless whether it is wood or metal.

• When not in use, keep the racket in a protective cover at the courts. After use, a racket press is the place to store the racket.

• You can enjoy more games from each ball if you store them in the refrigerator (do not freeze), and brush the dirt off the nap with a small brush.

TENTS, AWNINGS AND FLIES

• Always follow the manufacturer's instructions concerning methods of erection. This will prevent undue strain on important seams and other parts.

• Never store your tent while it is wet or even merely damp. Mildew will surely follow. If you must pack a wet tent, dry it out the first opportunity you get. Carry wooden poles outside the tent bag because wood absorbs moisture and can cause a trail of mildew on the tent.

• Always carry a tent repair kit with you in the woods. This will enable you to take care of small rips and tears as they occur and prevent them from becoming more serious.

• A tent with a built-in floor will accumulate a lot of debris. Make it a habit to keep the inside of the tent as clean as possible during use, and to clean it thoroughly once you get it home.

• Like tents, awnings or flies should not be rolled up while wet.

• Your camping dealer will tell you the best waterproofing compound to use on a particular piece of canvas or fabric. Renewing the waterproofing on such outdoor articles will give you more years of service than you may have thought possible.

While we haven't been able to cover every conceivable type of recreational equipment in this brief space, the techniques suggested above are easily adaptable to just about anything you work or play with. If a little time is spent on such equipment, and minor repairs are made as needed, it will repay you with long, enjoyable service.

Chapter 12

Miscellaneous Outdoor Equipment:

How to protect your big investments.

If you take a moment to look outside your window, you'll probably be amazed at the amount of money you've invested in your "outdoors." Apart from landscaping, trees and lawns, you may have a swimming pool or tennis court, children's play equipment, long runs of fencing, or other investments whose useful life can be prolonged with a little care.

In this chapter we will cover the more common items normally found outdoors. The general hints we give you here should not only enable you to take proper care of the specific things we mention, but also give you the background in good maintenance techniques that you can apply to many other things we couldn't possibly cover within the pages of a single book.

Gym sets. Proper maintenance of children's outdoor gym sets is important for two big reasons: First, this expensive piece of play equipment can be made to last all through your child's growing-up years; and second, your child's safety depends on proper maintenance. Fortunately, the job is not hard to do.

• Gym sets are usually made of steel tubing that is painted with outdoor enamel. Some parts, such as slides, may be galvanized to prevent rust. The first step in preventing rust is to keep the finish intact. While it is impossible to expect children to treat their play gym carefully as they do their indoor furniture, encourage them to be careful about scratching the finish. In other words, tell them not to ride their bikes deliberately into the gym set!

• Most gym sets are sold unassembled as packages of assorted tubes and hardware items. Be careful of the finish when unpacking and assembling the unit. If you do scratch the finish down to the bare metal, spray some clear lacquer on the spot to prevent rust from developing as soon as the set is put up.

• Spread a thin layer of clear white grease on hinge pins and other bearing surfaces where parts rub against each other. Not only will this prevent rust in the joints, but a lot of squeaks will also be eliminated.

• Spend the time and effort to mount the gym set properly. The main supports should be anchored in concrete which should come slightly above the level of the ground. This will make the set firm, sturdy, and safe for active children. It will also help prevent rust from starting at the bottom of the supports as will surely happen if they simply rest on the ground.

• Slides will work better and last longer if the surfaces are lightly waxed. A good way to do this is to crumple up a wad of waxed paper from the kitchen and then rub it all over the slide.

• Wooden parts, such as swing seats, should be painted regularly, *before* the paint has been worn off completely.

Sand boxes. This enjoyable play item usually becomes an eyesore after a short while. A little care can make it last longer for the kids and still not be something you would rather be rid of.

• Place some patio blocks, bricks, slates or flat planks around the outside of the sandbox extending about two feet all around. You can't keep the kids from spilling sand over the sides; but you can make it easy to sweep up and return to the sandbox.

• Cover the sandbox when not in use. This will keep small animals and pets from using the sandbox as a litterbox.

• If the sandbox is made of wood, be prepared to paint it at least once each season. Sand is an abrasive and quickly wears off a finish.

Tennis courts. A tennis court of your own can be a great source of enjoyment over the years. Because of the expense of installation, it is important that you maintain it properly in order to get the most out of this big investment.

All sorts of materials have been used for courts, each having certain advantages and disadvantages. Many home courts are constructed of a claylike material. Courts that are subjected to hard use, as in schools and public parks, are generally made of an all-weather surface, such as an asphaltic compound. In some areas of the country, concrete has been used for all-weather courts. Famous championship courts are grass, and in some countries, even wood has been used.

• Clay courts are inexpensive compared with all-weather surfaces, but the court requires daily care for best results.

• Every day, or after each day of play, the court should be dragged, watered and rolled. A good dragging tool can be made from three stiff push-brooms fastened together with strips of wood to form an extra wide broom. Brush this back and forth across the court to level out depressions and to fill in small footholes. Then water the court lightly, and roll firm with a court roller.

• Only tennis shoes should be permitted on the court. Other types of footwear will quickly ruin the surface.

• Don't play on the clay court right after a rain. Let the water drain for a day to permit the surface to firm up.

Asphaltic, "all-weather" courts are more expensive to install, but maintenance chores are very much reduced.

• Proper installation is necessary for long life. If you're getting such a court installed, make sure you deal with an experienced court builder. Get a guarantee in writing.

• Watch out for the hairline cracks in the surface. Water will freeze in the cracks and ultimately ruin the surface. Cracks should be filled with special court sealer, which is similar in action to a sealer used on driveways.

• Depressions which collect water should be filled and leveled by adding more material to fill the "saucer" and then sealing the whole surface to cover the patch.

• Sweep and hose the surface regularly to keep it free from debris.

A grass court is the ultimate luxury. If you want to go this route, be prepared for endless maintenance.

• Get good advice from a professional groundskeeper in your area as to the type of grass to use.

• Be prepared for constant re-seeding, grubbing, fertilizing, mowing and other chores to maintain a top playing surface.

Swimming pools. The most common pool found in the yard is the above-ground pool. This is usually considered a temporary pool, even though there may be an elaborate installation of accessory equipment—filters, ladders, heaters, and the like. A permanent in-ground pool is almost always installed by a professional pool builder.

Regardless of the type of pool you own, maintaining the water will be your biggest job. This often becomes a chore and is neglected, or is done improperly, with the result that the water is never as pure and inviting as it should be. If you will take a few moments to understand what happens to the water in your pool, you'll find that maintaining the water in top condition all the time isn't as burdensome as you thought.

The first thing you will need is a pool testing kit. This is available at all pool supply dealers, and is a must. Don't dose your pool with chemicals by guesswork; only the kit will tell you what are the proper chemical levels.

A variety of pool chemicals will be needed, and they can be purchased at the same place. At first, you may find all the different chemicals confusing, but they are simple to understand and use when you learn what each does.

Chlorination. Bacteria will quickly grow in untreated water, and will spread infection and disease from one swimmer to another. Chlorine is the chemical used to disinfect the water by killing harmful bacteria. It comes in various forms such as powders and tablets.

• Use your pool testing kit to determine chlorine level; it should be adjusted to 1.0 parts per million. Too little chlorine won't protect you, while too much will be harmful and irritating to your nose, throat, and eyes.

• Test for chlorine level both in the morning and in the evening. Sunlight causes a rapid loss of chlorine so that a pool that is safe in the morning may have less than the recommended 1.0 parts per million in the afternoon.

• Adding a chlorine stabilizer will help prevent loss of chlorine.

• Don't over-chlorinate your pool with the thought that you will save future work. You'll only succeed in making every swimmer uncomfortable.

pH level. The peculiar symbol *pH* is the scientist's way of describing and measuring the acidity or alkalinity of any fluid, including swimming pool water. Pure, neutral water measures 7.0 on the pH scale. It is neither acid or alkaline. If the water has a pH rating below 7.0 (such as 6.5 or 5.2) it is considered acid. A pH rating above 7.0 (such as 7.8 or 8.3) is considered alkaline. The ideal range for swimming pool water is between 7.4 and 7.8. This is moderately alkaline and is found to be most comfortable to swimmers.

• Use your pool testing kit to measure pH level every day, preferably in the morning. Use the proper chemical recommended by your dealer to raise or lower the pH until it falls in the range of 7.4 to 7.8.

• Any chlorine product you use in your pool will work better and last longer if you maintain this pH level.

• High pH can lead to skin irritations, while low levels can cause reddening of eyes and discomfort to the mucous membranes.

• Filters, piping and other pool equipment will be attacked by pool water which is acid, or below 7.0 on you pH test scale.

Algae control. Algae are microscopic plants that are found everywhere. They will grow quickly in a pool warmed by the sun. In no time at all, the surface will be covered with a slimy green coating.

• Preventive maintenance is the best course of action. When filling your pool, add an algaecide to prevent future growth of these plants.

• If algae do gain a foothold, more drastic treatment will be needed. Ask your dealer for a special one-shot chemical designed for this purpose.

• Use an algaecide throughout the season at the rate recommended for the size pool you own.

In certain areas of the country, the water contains large amounts of iron, manganese, copper, or calcium salts which cause discoloration and cloudiness in the water. Your pool supply dealer will know what the local problems are and no doubt has special chemicals for the particular condition in your locale. Take his advice.

Once you know all the chemicals and their uses, make yourself a checklist divided into weeks. Put this near the pool and use it to make sure you add the right chemical, at the right time, and in the right amount. A simple system such as this will go a long way toward eliminating the "chore" aspect of maintaining proper water quality, and will pay big dividends in safe, healthful, and enjoyable swimming.

Vinyl pool maintenance. With a little extra care, you can get a lot more life out of your vinyl pool than you may have thought possible.

• Proper installation will increase pool life significantly. Make sure the pool rests on a level base, such as a sand bed. If you leave sharp stones under the liner, you're asking for early trouble.

• The frame should be square and level. If the sides tilt, the weight of the water will make the problem worse. Again, this is an installation problem that should be handled correctly at the beginning.

• Use a vinyl pool cleaner to remove encrusted soil, sun-tan oils, and other forms of unsightly dirt.

• Take care of pin hole leaks at once before they get bigger. Pool dealers carry vinyl pool repair kits that can be used under water.

Concrete pool maintenance. Getting a concrete pool ready takes some time to do properly. Therefore, you should start very early in the Spring. Usually, the three jobs to be done are cleaning, repairing minor cracks, and painting.

• Drain the water and remove leaves, dirt and other debris. Loose or scaling paint should be thoroughly scraped. Sweep out the dirt carefully so it doesn't wind up in your filtering or pumping system.

• Cracks and expansion joints should be filled with patching or sealing compound. A large settlement crack probably needs the attention of an expert.

• Concrete pools should be etched with muriatic acid, using one gallon of acid to three gallons of water. You should use about a gallon of this diluted solution per 100 square feet of pool surface. Do the sides and the bottom of the pool. Rinse with plenty of water and let dry thoroughly.

• Paint the pool with a chlorinated rubber base paint. Make sure the pool is really dry before you paint, and try not to paint in direct, hot sunlight. Don't paint when the temperature is below 50 degrees or above 90 degrees Fahrenheit.

When the swimming season finally ends, take a little time to close down the pool properly. Time spent on this last chore will save you hours and hours of work the following year when you want to start swimming again.

Recirculating equipment. This includes filters, pumps, and piping that can be damaged by freeze-ups.

• Filters should be thoroughly backwashed and completely drained. If any repairs have to be made, do them at this time.

• The pump should be drained and greased. At the same time, you should also remove the fuse controlling the pump so it can't be turned on accidentally without any water in it.

• Feeding and chlorination equipment should be completely drained and all parts lubricated to prevent corrosion during the winter.

The pool. Apart from the maintenance details already covered, there are several other steps necessary to winterize your pool.

• An ice-control pillow should be placed in the pool as a protection against ice thrust. Don't drain an in-ground pool for the winter; without the support of the water against the sides, the pool can be severely damaged by the ground heaving in cold weather.

• A pool cover should be used to prevent the accumulation of winter debris.

• Special chemicals can be added to give the pool long-term protection against the formation of slime and odors during the winter months.

The pool area. The final step in winterizing your pool is to take care of pool equipment and swimming gear.

• All deck equipment such as chairs, diving boards, ladders, and the like should be stored properly. Diving boards should be laid on a flat surface to prevent warping.

• The water supply should be shut off and all fixtures drained.

• The electrical system should be deactivated by removing all fuses.

• The pool cabins or changing areas should be cleaned of towels, suits and other swimming articles. Bathing caps, sunglasses and combs will not be of much use if left out all year.

• A swimming pool requires a great deal of attention compared with other recreational installations. However, if you familiarize yourself with the steps needed to keep a pool in top-notch shape, and then follow a definite schedule of checking and treating the water, you should get hours of enjoyment from your pool without the discouragement that always accompanies hit-or-miss maintenance techniques.

Fences. Virtually every building material has been used for the construction of fences, so it is impossible to give recommendations for every type. However, a few general principles apply and will enable you to get more years of life out of your fence.

• Stone and masonry fences are the most durable, and little care is needed to keep them in good shape. If mortar is used to fill joints between bricks or stones, it should be checked once a year for cracking. Loose mortar should be pointed or replaced with a pre-packaged mortar mix available in any hardware store.

• Wooden fences have a limited life which can be extended with proper care. Board or plank fences should be kept painted and in good repair.

• Rustic fencing should be protected with a wood preservative at regular intervals.

• If wooden fence posts are placed in the ground directly, the ends should be pretreated with wood preservative before installation. This will add years to the life of a post.

• Shovel some dirt around each fence post in the Spring, and then tamp it firmly down. This will tighten the post in the ground and prevent the fence from falling over in a light wind.

• If at all possible, install fence posts in concrete bases that come up slightly above ground level. This will prevent decay and also make the post much more sturdy.

• Metal fencing, such as chain link fencing, should be installed by someone experienced in such matters. A proper job of installation will make the fence last longer and look better.

• If the fence is galvanized steel, watch for wear of the rust-proof coating after some years. Before the fence begins to rust, give it a coat of paint. Special paint rollers make the job easy to do.

• Metal gates, hinges, and other moving parts should be lubricated with white grease. This prevents undue wear and squeaks.

• Discourage children from climbing fences. After a while a sag will develop which is impossible to eliminate.

Other outdoor equipment. No one book could possibly hope to cover every article found in use outdoors. However, some general principles can be given which will apply to just about anything. Common sense will provide the rest of the information you need. Here are some things to keep in mind:

• Anything exposed to the elements outdoors will wear much more rapidly than a similar item inside. A baked enamel finish on a kitchen appliance will look good for many years indoors. The same finish on an outdoor article will wear in a season or two. Therefore, anything left outdoors should be inspected frequently and minor repair or touch-up jobs done promptly to avoid bigger headaches later on.

• Outdoor items get dirty much faster, so cleaning is needed more frequently. If you neglect to clean an outdoor grill, for example, in no time at all the article or unit will become unsightly, and probably work less efficiently.

• Remember that northern winters are hard on anything that has to be left outdoors. The first thing you should do in early Spring is to make a thorough inspection for winter damage and do the necessary repairs. Once you get into summer, you will probably be involved in other chores and be inclined to let things go. A second winter can ruin something completely.

If you follow the directions we've given in the previous pages, you'll find that with relatively few hours a week invested in maintenance chores, you'll have many more hours left over to enjoy your recreational equipment and installations—or simply have the satisfaction of seeing your grounds in great shape year after year.

Index